PRINCI▮▮▮

of

WAR

for the

CORPORATE
BATTLEFIELD

WARFIGHTING LESSONS
for BUSINESS LEADERS

MIKE ETTORE
U.S. MARINE CORPS (RETIRED)

Fidelis Leadership Group
Developing World Class Leaders

Principles of War for the Corporate Battlefield
Warfighting Lessons for Business Leaders

Paperback ISBN: 978-0-9898229-9-2
Hardcover ISBN: 978-1-7372881-0-7
Ebook ISBN: 978-1-7372881-1-4

CONTENTS

COVER EXPLANATION

In Greek mythology, Hector, the oldest child of King Priam and Hecuba, was the presumed heir to the throne of Troy. He was regarded as the greatest Trojan hero of the Trojan War, the main defender of Troy, and a favorite of the god, Apollo.

As described in Homer's *The Iliad*, Hector came very close to winning the war for the Trojans during a period of time when the legendary warrior, Achilles temporarily deserted the Greeks. Hector capitalized on this opportunity, stormed the Greek camp and with Apollo's help, killed Achilles' best friend, Patroclus, and stole his armor, which actually belonged to Achilles.

Enraged by the death of his friend, Achilles rejoined the Greeks in fighting against the Trojans in order to pursue Hector. As the Greeks attacked the Trojan castle, Hector came out to meet Achilles in single combat—wearing the armor he'd taken off the body of Patroclus. Achilles knew where the vulnerabilities of this set of armor were located, and he aimed and shot his spear into a small gap in the neck area of that armor, killing Hector.

Afterward, Achilles desecrated Hector's corpse by dragging it around the grave of Patroclus three times, and several times around the outer walls of Troy. King Priam, Hector's father, then went to Achilles to beg for his son's body so he could give it a proper burial. Despite the abuse of the corpse at the hands of the Greeks, Hector's body had been kept intact due to the intervention of the gods.

The Iliad ends with the funeral of Hector, held during a 12-day truce granted by Achilles.

Application to Business Leadership

In modern warfare, the desecration of the bodies of dead enemy soldiers is considered to be dishonorable and for American warriors, a criminal act that will result in severe punishment.

However, in the business world, the ramifications of ill-advised decisions and directives by arrogant or inept leaders often results in their companies being "dragged around the city of Troy" for all to see. One way leaders can minimize the chances of this happening is to leverage lessons and best practices from various sources and apply them to their own environment.

To this end, I urge leaders to study the time-tested Principles of War covered in this book and integrate them into their business planning and operations. I've used them with great effect both as a combat leader and as a C-level executive in a publicly traded company.

Fidelis Leadership Group
Developing World Class Leaders

—Principles of War—

Objective

Offensive

Mass

Economy of Force

Maneuver

Unity of Command

Security

Surprise

Simplicity

INTRODUCTION

No other human endeavor matches the intensity, fluidity, and violence of warfare—and the life and death stakes of success or failure. But modern business and war have much in common. Many military concepts and lessons learned on countless battlefields throughout history can be successfully applied to business leadership, strategic planning, and operational tactics and techniques.

The "Business Battlefield" is a competition that can sometimes become so fierce that it approaches a zero-sum game. There are battles with clear winners and losers, survivors and the vanquished. Resources must be allocated rapidly and intelligently. Highly coordinated teamwork is essential. And success depends on leaders who can make quick, smart and effective decisions in complex and rapidly changing environments.

Business leaders often speak in military metaphors, using words like "air cover," "surgical strike," and, of course, terms such as "strategy, tactics and execution." Business schools teach the ideas espoused by great military thinkers like the Chinese General Sun Tzu and the Prussian General Carl von Clausewitz. Some schools instruct students to wargame policies to fight the modern-day Islamic State or teach how lessons from warfare apply to conflict resolution and leadership. [1] [2] [3]

The objectives and strategies defined by major corporations are often crafted in a manner similar to that associated with large-scale military operations. In the 1960s, for example, Canon attacked Xerox's dominant position in the copier industry. The upstart company outflanked its enemy by taking new ground—untapped market share. Xerox implemented a novel, highly-successful strategy targeting small businesses and selling rather than leasing machines. And decades later, Xerox renewed its battle against its rival with a simple slogan: "Beat Canon." [4] [5]

1

During the "Cola Wars" of the 1980s, Pepsi relentlessly chipped away at Coca-Cola's lead in soft drinks. Both companies employed a series of product roll-outs and aggressive marketing campaigns that resembled battles. "The Pepsi Challenge," an ad campaign that showed Pepsi winning blind taste tests, was an early victory for the challenger. The subsequent introduction of "New Coke"—an attempt to match the sweeter, preferred taste of Pepsi—was a tactical failure by Coca-Cola. But it ended up as a strategic victory for the reigning soft-drink champ. Consumer backlash spurred by brand loyalty caused the company to reintroduce "Classic Coke," and the venerable brand rode a wave of financial success that reasserted dominance over its rival.[6]

So, while business isn't war, it can certainly be *a form of competition that I often refer to as "bloodless combat."* Today's business leaders can learn a great deal from a few thousand years of armed conflict and martial philosophy. In particular, **The Nine Principles of War** offer crucial lessons for business leaders. Perhaps no other piece of military doctrine or philosophy is as broadly useful, or so straightforwardly sums up **how to maximize the chances for business success**.

The Nine Principles of War

There are numerous versions of and sources for these enduring principles. British Major-General John Frederick Charles "Boney" Fuller is credited with creating several modern forms of the list just before and after World War I. The U.S. Army modified and officially adopted one of his lists in 1925. However, some version of these principles had been taught at the United States Military Academy at West Point since the early 19th Century. And while every list includes ideas that have many fathers—including Sun Tzu, Clausewitz, and the Renaissance philosopher Niccolò Machiavelli—the modern principles are often attributed to Baron Antoine Henri de Jomini.

Jomini was a French-Swiss officer who fought for the Swiss, French, and Russian armies; and famously served under Napoleon Bonaparte during the Napoleonic Wars. He was also a prolific writer about military strategy whose work was intensely studied by 19th Century militaries, including the U.S. Army. Jomini is perhaps most well-known for the idea that there is "a list of general truths whose application contributes to success in war." [7] [8]

Today, the U.S. military still uses The Nine Principles of War, as featured in the *U.S. Army Field Manual (FM) 3-0 Operations* and the *U.S. Marine Corps Doctrinal Publication (MCDP) 1 Warfighting.*

The Nine Principles of War are:

1. **Objective:** Direct every military operation toward a clearly defined, decisive, and attainable objective.

2. **Offensive:** Seize, retain, and exploit the initiative.

3. **Mass:** Concentrate the effects of combat power at the decisive place and time.

4. **Economy of Force:** Allocate minimum essential combat power to secondary efforts.

5. **Maneuver:** Place the enemy in a disadvantageous position through the flexible application of combat power.

6. **Unity of Command:** For every objective, ensure unity of effort under one responsible commander.

7. **Security:** Never permit the enemy to acquire an unexpected advantage.

8. **Surprise:** Strike the enemy at a time or place or in a manner for which he is unprepared.

9. **Simplicity:** Prepare clear, uncomplicated plans and clear, concise orders to ensure thorough understanding. [9]

I detail these principles in subsequent chapters but think of how each can apply in both the military and business worlds. Take **mass** and **objective**, for example.

During the Operation Desert Shield/Desert Storm, a multinational coalition of nearly a million troops **massed** against about 650,000 Iraqi troops. Supported and preceded by a stunning air campaign that conducted 109,876 sorties in 43 days—"an average of 2,555 sorties per day"— the ground invasion accomplished the war's "clearly defined, decisive, and attainable **objective**" in just 100 hours: expel the Iraqi Army from Kuwait.[10]

In 1923, former Coca-Cola President and Chairman Robert Woodruff set an **objective** that a Coke should be "Within an arm's reach of desire." Essentially, every human being on the planet should be able to buy the soft drink, whenever and wherever they wanted it. The company has largely made good on this goal in the past century with **mass** production, marketing, and distribution efforts. Coca-Cola now sells about 1.8 billion bottles per day to a global population of 7.8 billion people.[11]

Consider how **maneuver**, **economy of force**, and **simplicity** match up with any business's quest for specialization, a well-defined market, and a Unique Selling Proposition (USP). An auto repair shop that services European imports doesn't waste expertise, time, and money by working on Chevys, instead of focusing its "combat power" and resources on a profitable niche market. And, while Michelin may be a French multinational that has mildly diversified into maps and travel guides, its core focus remains manufacturing and selling tires—to the tune of almost $1.9 billion in net revenue per year.[12]

Surprise and **security** hold obvious and incredibly relevant lessons for modern businesses that face challenges from unexpected quarters. Wal-Mart challenged and defeated Sears with a convenient, lower-cost, all-things-to-all-customers model, and Amazon has now significantly disrupted Wal-Mart. The hotel industry didn't quickly perceive or react to the threat from Airbnb, and Uber and Lyft have almost completely conquered the traditional taxi industry.

Beyond overall business strategy, these principles also apply to daily operations and individual leadership. Both businesses and militaries must operate in complex environments and marshal a wide range of resources. The combined arms concept of a military campaign calls for supporting infantry and other ground forces with the timely and coordinated employment of airpower, artillery and other supporting arms, logistics, and other resources. Likewise, to be effective, business leaders must master the effective application of marketing, sales, distribution, operations, administration, and various elements associated with human resources.

Both business and war intensely depend on teamwork. The organizations that achieve the most success have a clear chain of command, but individual units that work together while having the latitude to adapt within their sphere of influence. The military and corporate worlds each need well-trained leaders at all levels who can make smart decisions to propel the organization forward. Successful companies and units rely on decentralized command and control, which, of course, is based upon the existence of a culture of trust that exists at every level of the organization.

There are countless similarities between military concepts and methodologies and the world of business, and much can be learned from studying the masters of war in order to master business operations. Read on to learn how The Nine Principles of War can help you become a better leader, planner, and decision-maker.

OBJECTIVE

Direct every operation towards a clearly defined, decisive, and attainable objective.

As I write this chapter, the United States has been fighting a war in Afghanistan for 19 years, the longest conflict in American history. The US military has contended with a committed and robust insurgency, difficult geography, and a lack of viable local government partners, among other challenges. But perhaps the biggest roadblock to success is the failure of senior American political and military leaders to define an adequate **objective**.

Was the objective to seek justice for the terrorist attacks on September 11, 2001? To capture or kill Osama bin Laden, al Qaeda's then-emir and the architect of the attacks? To defeat and remove the Taliban, which sheltered al Qaeda? To build a democratic government in Afghanistan? To deny terrorist groups a staging area from which to conduct more worldwide attacks?

The objective has been all of these things and more. And while analysts debate the extent to which the US has succeeded or failed to hit any of these goals, it's clear that our government has dropped the ball in one respect: to outline an objective that meets the standards of The Nine Principles of War.

The military goal or "desired end state" in Afghanistan was never "clearly defined," in fact, it seemed to change every couple of years or so. And nearly two decades of effort have shown that some of these goals were neither "decisive" nor "attainable." Two presidential administrations have actively sought to remove US troops while achieving some durable—or, at least, acceptable—outcome.

Contrast that conflict with the first war with Iraq: Operations Desert Shield and Desert Storm. After Iraqi President Saddam Hussein ordered his troops to invade and occupy Kuwait in August 1990 and began menacing Saudi Arabia, the US assembled a multinational military coalition to stage in the Arabian Peninsula. Conducted between August 1990 – January 1991, Operation Desert Shield had the "clearly defined, decisive, and attainable objective" of stopping Iraq's military expansion. It transitioned into Operation Desert Storm, which had the sole objective of expelling the Iraqi military from Kuwait. This outcome was decisively achieved in 43 days, after a sustained bombing campaign and a 100-hour ground invasion. [13] [14]

Of all of the Principles of War, objective is probably the most easily understood and relatable for business leaders. Everyone agrees with its fundamental premise, and every business school, system, and coach and consultant espouses the need for clear targets. A commonly used civilian version of this principle is the idea of setting SMART goals, which are:

- Specific
- Measurable
- Attainable
- Relevant
- Time-based

Many business leaders, however, still have trouble defining and implementing a good objective. The difficulty lies in both identifying one *and* evaluating and coordinating resources to make it attainable and decisive. Here is how the Marine Corps expands on these factors when training new officers:

> Related to mass and economy of force, we must know where
> to mass and where to economize, which is defined by a

decisive objective. It is also related to unity of command, as each subordinate must be led by the intent of one command-er, towards the commonly defined objective. Communication is also critical, ensuring that the elements of the military oper-ation are acting in consonance towards the same end. [15]

Note that the Principles of War act in concert—there is an active and respon-sive feedback loop between principles. Objective, however, is the principle from which all others usually flow.

It's also important to understand that an objective doesn't just apply to or-ganizations' overall goals, but every level, department, and individual. The basics of clearly identifying an objective that is decisive and attainable work equally well for the five-year goal of a Fortune 500 company and the quarter-ly targets of an individual employee.

Business Objectives: The Bad

Yahoo! was the most visited site in the world at the turn of the century, and where most internet users started their day online. Two decades later, how-ever, the company barely cracks the top 10. It has stagnated into a shadow of its former self and become an also-ran to tech giants like Google and Facebook. This decline serves as an excellent example of failing to implement a proper objective. [16]

Yahoo! started as a human-built directory of websites "organized in a hi-erarchical way"—in contrast to the search engines we use today, which automatically aggregate and rank all sites. Nevertheless, the internet was young, and there were far fewer websites, so the company quickly solidified itself as the go-to portal. Yahoo! failed to capitalize on this success, however:

- The exponential growth of the internet made its human-indexed web directory unsustainable, and the company failed to invest early in modern search engine technology.

- Yahoo! went on a buying spree of over 100 acquisitions over the ensu-ing decades, including web hosting services, internet service providers, and media outlets such as internet radio stations, fantasy sports sites, social media, movie and music services, financial information sites, and more. The company even finally bought a search engine, though it eventually handed off that service to a partnership with Google. Yahoo! followed up many of these purchases by failing to "[integrate] them into its ecosystem." [17] [18] [19]

- The company did not recognize and capitalize on the rise of modern search engines and social media at the early phases of adoption, turning down deals to buy both Google and Facebook. Yahoo!'s efforts to launch or acquire and integrate various platforms often failed or encountered severe challenges. The company also suffered a hack that compromised more than three billion user accounts in 2013. [20] [21]

If you've read my previous book, *Trust-Based Leadership™: Marine Corps Leadership Concepts for Today's Business Leaders*, you will be familiar with the importance of *commander's intent*. The Trust-Based Leadership model's success is hugely contingent on a clearly and concisely stated intent—what it is that you as a company are trying to achieve. The failure to clearly define what Yahoo's mission and intent were is evidence of poor leadership. In many respects, Yahoo!'s failure to leverage its status as an internet leader stems from a muddy objective. Is it a web directory? A search engine? A media company? A social media company? An entertainment provider? An internet service provider?

The answer: Yahoo! is basically a website with a lot of traffic—and a company with immense resources—that strived to be all of the above, to one degree or another.

This lack of focus—of a clear, decisive, and attainable objective—resulted in being too many things to too many people. It spurred failure to capitalize on trends that have morphed companies like Google and Facebook into the new internet titans. As early as 2005, *Wired* writer Michael Malone observed that "it's just not easy to say what Yahoo! is." [22]

Much like the war in Afghanistan, it's hard to pin down Yahoo!'s objective.

Yahoo! is certainly not the only example. Formerly great companies such as Kmart, Toys"R"Us, Toshiba, Sears, Blockbuster, and Blackberry all stumbled because they failed to innovate or set achievable objectives. They lacked goals that would enable them to remain relevant, take advantage of opportunities, and achieve decisive wins.

Business Objectives: The Good

In contrast, the objective of a company like Warby Parker is clear. Launched in 2010, the online retailer has "the sole purpose of providing people with designer prescription glasses." By 2018, it had grown to over 90 locations, more than 1,700 employees, and a $1.7 billion valuation. [23] [24]

PayPal has remained focused on online money transfers and payment processing, an objective reflected in its mission statement: "To build the web's most convenient, secure, cost-effective payment solution." The company has enjoyed steady growth, increasing from just over $3.4 billion in net revenue in 2010 to $17.8 billion in 2019. [25] [26]

And while CEO Elon Musk has his hands in numerous projects and companies, "Tesla's mission is to accelerate the world's transition to sustainable energy." The company seems poised to achieve this goal, having "shifted the auto industry toward electric vehicles and achieved consistently growing revenues (passing $20 billion in 2019). At the start of 2020, Tesla was the highest performing automaker in terms of total return, sales growth and long-term shareholder value." [27]

High-performing companies may eventually stumble if they stray from their objective or fail to adapt it, when necessary. But this fundamental **Principle of War** remains vital for any military or business endeavor: identify, set, and work to define and achieve clear **objectives** to achieve overall success. It is the principle from which all others flow.

> *"If a man does not know to what port he is steering,*
> *no wind is favorable."*
>
> —SENECA

2

Offensive

Seize, retain, and exploit the initiative.

"The best defense is a good offense," is another way of expressing this Principle of War—one recognized by strategists throughout the ages.

"Attack is the secret of defense; defense is the planning of an attack," wrote famous Chinese strategist Sun Tzu in *The Art of War*.

"[O]ffensive operations, often times, is the surest, if not the only (in some cases) means of defense," wrote George Washington, commenting on how to deal with Napoleon's intent of reestablishing French territory in North America. [28] [29]

The **offensive** principle relies on continually moving forward—on the attack—toward your goal, whatever it is. In combat, that often means seizing, clearing, or otherwise controlling key terrain and other objectives that can help to defeat an enemy force. In business, it means always pressing the advantage to meet objectives, whether they are the completion of a project, opening a new line of services, or taking market share from competitors. Staying offensive does not involve neglecting defense—it merely means using defense as a tool *in service of offense*.

The Marine Corps explains this concept to new officers as follows:

> Maintaining an offensive mindset does not imply that we seek to avoid defense. Rather it implies the use of the defense as a temporary expedient to prepare to resume the offense. Offense being the decisive form of combat, it is the method by which we exploit the enemy vulnerability, impose our will, and determine the course of war. [30]

With rare exceptions—such as a disastrous frontal attack by an enemy on a fortified position or weathering an industry-wide crisis that destroys competitors—defense doesn't win battles or achieve objectives. And even when a strong defense comes close, offensive operations must still resume to exploit the aftermath and solidify victory.

Offense in a Seemingly Defensive Situation

By 2006, the second war in Iraq was not going well for the U.S. military. Despite a quick "conventional victory" after the 2003 invasion, a strong insurgency had developed and was wreaking havoc on coalition attempts to stabilize the country. In the city of Fallujah in the western province of Anbar, the situation was particularly dangerous and unpredictable. A coalition of nationalist rebels and radical religious extremists loosely cooperated to attack Americans and the Iraqi government.

In a sense, the insurgents set the pace of the conflict. They could blend into the local population and use guerilla tactics to attack at times and places of their choosing. Snipers, improvised explosive devices (IEDs), mortars, and other hit-and-run attacks were common. U.S. forces were placed in a defensive posture as they attempted to back up Iraqi security forces that would lead the fight.

In early 2007, however, the strategy changed. President George W. Bush announced a "surge" of troops in January, and a new commanding general, David Petraeus, implemented a comprehensive counterinsurgency (COIN) strategy aimed at stabilizing the country. The objective of COIN is to provide enough security and stability to win the cooperation of a critical mass of local citizens, who then assist the security forces in defeating the insurgency.

It involves many defensive aspects. Counterinsurgents in Iraq had to protect territory, civilians, and government officials while helping local security forces. Nevertheless, the U.S. military's application of the doctrine unquestionably relied on relentless *offense*.

In Fallujah, U.S. Marines "attacked" the city—neighborhood by neighborhood—that spring. In operations dubbed "the Swarm," a force of Marines, Iraqi soldiers, and Iraqi police rolled into a specific community, fought any insurgents who decided to fight, and fortified the area with checkpoints. They established local police and military headquarters, gathered a council of local leaders to assess needs, and provided civil assistance, including food, supplies, medical care, and infrastructure improvements. Security forces stayed in each neighborhood to maintain security. As civilians began to feel safe, they often provided some information about the insurgents—who had previously ruthlessly run the communities. And as more and more areas were "swarmed," this smattering of intelligence turned into a ton.

At the same time, a punishing offensive against the insurgents took place behind the scenes of the main effort. U.S. Special Operations forces, along with local and conventional U.S. forces, conducted relentless raids on insurgent leaders and cells in and around the city. Night after night, U.S. and Iraqi troops would go out into the city's neighborhoods or outskirts and capture or kill insurgents—bleeding these groups' manpower and leadership.

The offensive pressure was constant and effective. When this effort was coupled with securing neighborhoods and newly empowered local security forces, the insurgents were largely driven out of Fallujah.

This is a good example of the **offensive** principle because it illustrates how it applies in a seemingly defensive situation. U.S. and Iraqi forces had to focus on protecting themselves and civilians to achieve the **objective**, but never relinquished an offensive posture during the effort.

They seized the initiative by entering neighborhoods, retained it by securing areas and gathering intelligence, and exploited it by applying the information to put constant pressure on the enemy. While Fallujah would descend into chaos again after U.S. withdrawal, one of the most insecure cities in Iraq enjoyed relative peace for years after these operations.

Business Offensives

Perhaps no other company has maintained an offensive posture as relentlessly as Amazon. While widely known as an e-commerce giant, it has expanded into just about everything with a digital aspect:

> It's now the largest provider of cloud computing services and a maker of home security systems. Amazon is a fashion designer, advertising business, television and movie producer, book publisher, and the owner of a sprawling platform for crowdsourced micro-labor tasks. The company now occupies roughly as much space worldwide as 38 Pentagons. [31]

From its modest origins as an online bookseller 26 years ago, Amazon has extended its reach into nearly every aspect of daily life:

> Amazon is now America's second-largest private employer. (Walmart is the largest.) It traffics more than a third of all retail products bought or sold online in the U.S.; it owns Whole Foods and helps arrange the shipment of items purchased across the Web, including on eBay and Etsy. Amazon's Web-services division powers vast portions of the Internet, from Netflix to the C.I.A. [32]

The online behemoth has achieved this status with intensive growth strategies revolving around market development, market penetration, product development, and diversification. While the company has had its share of missteps—such as the Fire (Smart) Phone, a digital wallet, and a travel booking site—it has quickly retrenched from any failures while constantly expanding into new and profitable territory.

The best way to describe the company's overall strategy is "relentlessly offensive." In fact, Jeff Bezos almost named the company "Relentless," and Amazon "still owns the URL for relentless.com—it redirects you to Amazon. com." Amazon has weathered criticism over its dominance, reach, and labor practices—but no one can argue with its success. [33] [34]

There are numerous examples of companies that share this offensive mindset:

- Shopify's "share price is up by more than 1,000% since 2015" based on its differentiation from competitors and aggressive penetration into the e-commerce website development space.

- The NBA has expanded the popularity of professional basketball to an unprecedented degree worldwide, largely through streaming that "distributes its games and programming in 215 countries and territories and in fifty languages." [35]

- Domino's Pizza has seen an exponential increase in its share price—from $60 in 2013 to $377 in 2020—much of it based on aggressive technology innovation. The "first major pizza chain to introduce online and mobile ordering," Domino's instituted an online order tracker and is now pioneering self-driving delivery vehicles. [36] [37] [38]

Each of these companies has remained offensive, constantly devising and implementing new ways to take ground.

Focused Aggression and Action

The key to a successful military as well as business offensive is not merely relentless action. Instead, it is aggression in light of circumstances and always focused on a well-defined **objective**. Companies that chase growth in unsustainable sectors or product lines wind up with massive holes in their balance sheet. Those that press forward and forget their core objective, skillset, and purpose tend to spread thin their efforts and fail.

As with all of the **Principles of War**, **offensive** works in concert with others. Staying true to the **objective** is apparent, but **mass** and **maneuver**—intelligently and flexibly applying resources to the maximum point of impact—are also essential. **Economy of force** enables leaders to avoid devoting "combat power" to pointless offensives. And **security** emphasizes the role of defense in an effective offense. Just as an unchecked charge at an enemy can result in a disastrous ambush, prudent business decision-makers always assess their organizations' vulnerabilities before pressing ahead.

The essence of this principle works very well in business, where companies tend to grow or die. Move toward a clear objective by first identifying key opportunities—and then attack, attack, attack!

"I should say that in general the first of two army commanders who adopts an offensive attitude almost always reduces his rival to the defensive and makes him proceed in consonance with the movement of the former."

—FREDERICK THE GREAT

3

Mass

Concentrate the effects of combat power
at the decisive place and time.

The Civil War's Confederate General Nathan Bedford Forrest is a contro-versial historical figure , but he is widely recognized as having been an exceptional battlefield commander, and one worthy of study by military pro-fessionals as well as business leaders who are seeking concepts and lessons they can apply to their respective "business battlefields."

Forrest used innovative tactics and racked up a record of victories that caused Union General William Tecumseh Sherman to refer to him as "that Devil Forrest." In terms of military skill, Sherman considered the Confederate general "the most remarkable man our civil war produced on either side," and the historian Shelby Foote regarded Forrest as one of "two authentic geniuses" of the war (the other was Abraham Lincoln). [39] [40]

Forrest did not have a military education. Nevertheless, he described the principle of **mass** when he famously summed up his recipe for battlefield victory:

"Get there first with the most men." [41]

Mass is one of the most straightforward principles of war to understand, but it can be deceptively difficult to execute. Every military or business leader wants enough resources—be it troops, funds, manufacturing capacity, logistical support, or some other types of "supporting arms" —to strike at the decisive point and overwhelm "the enemy." The difficulty lies in deciding when, where, and how to apply that power.

In military terms, defining the enemy is often straightforward. In business, however, the "enemy" could be a rival company, a new or untapped market niche that presents an opportunity, or an essential expansion of existing services that generates efficiencies or revenue. The concept also applies to how you deploy all available resources, including the talented people on your team. A financial analyst who works well in isolation has very different "combat power" than a sales rep with incredible people skills, or an innovative executive who consistently comes up with new ideas. Whatever the application, *resources in any form must be deployed appropriately and in enough mass to "win."*

Effectively utilizing mass involves marshaling these resources and deciding where to use them. Here's how the U.S. Marine Corps explains these factors (**emphasis added**) to new officers:

> [W]e must first identify which factors are critical to the enemy, and then identify a relative vulnerability to that center of gravity – this is the enemy's critical vulnerability. Vital to the concept of mass is having the insight to identify the decisive place and time in which to attack the enemy's critical vulnerability. **Concentrated fire power is irrelevant if applied to an objective of no significance.** We seek mass to overwhelm the enemy in an attempt to deliver the decisive blow. ... It is closely related to economy of force, as force available is limited and we must decide when and where it is appropriate to mass or economize our force. [42]

As with other Principles of War, Mass does not exist in isolation. It works in tandem with a well-defined **objective** and appropriate **economy of force** and ideally involves **surprise**.

A good business example of applying Mass successfully—and then failing to use it well—is found in the whiplashing fortunes of General Electric Co. GE's modern eras are often divided into "Jack Welch" and "After Jack Welch."

The Jack Welch Era

When the former GE CEO took over the company in 1980, he changed its objective from "grow[ing] faster than the economy" to becoming "the world's most valuable company." Welch followed up on this **objective** with a **massed** attack on the corporation's existing culture, processes, and business lines that enabled a relentless campaign to grow the company and generate profits. [43]

Welch quickly started "blowing up the bureaucracy, eliminating the formalized meetings that had long marked GE's culture, and installing a blunter, more freewheeling style that prioritized 'facing realities' over 'superficial congeniality.'" He closed, sold, or fixed any business lines that weren't market leaders, purging 71 businesses in his first two years. Welch also instituted higher employee standards, conducted significant layoffs, and focused on expanding a promising revenue source: GE Capital, the company's lending arm, wound up yielding huge profits. [44]

Fortune writer Geoffrey Colvin described Welch's management style and changes as "blitzkrieg aggressiveness" and asserts that the CEO's "great achievement" was in clearly recognizing how the business world was changing. And "having seen it, [Welch] faced up to the huge, painful changes it demanded, and made them faster and more emphatically than anyone else in business." [45]

This is an excellent example of applying the principle of mass. Welch recognized an opportunity and the reality—"the decisive place and time"—and then concentrated the effects of 'combat power' to achieve GE's objective. During his tenure, the "company's revenue jumped nearly fivefold, to $130 billion ... while the value of its shares on the stock market soared from $14 billion to more than $410 billion." [46]

After Jack Welch

Jeff Immelt took over as CEO in 2001 and led GE for 16 years—a run that saw the company's stock lose roughly "38 percent of its value." The strategy he inherited from Welch had mostly run its course, and some of the moves the previous CEO championed had a role in the decline that followed. But Immelt's decisions were ultimately responsible for the company's performance, and many of them illustrate a poor application of mass. [47]

During Immelt's tenure, GE chased growth by expanding its credit business to represent 55% of revenue just before the Great Recession of 2008 hit—well above the generally accepted 40% cap during Welch's tenure. This increased focus on financial services significantly worsened the crisis's impact on the company.

Under Welch's previous leadership, GE had implemented an aggressive acquisition strategy that focused on buying successful "businesses ranked first or second in industries with only three or four players." But by 2001, this strategy had become less viable, as it had spawned a sea of imitators who competed for acquisitions and drove up sales prices. [48] [49]

Nevertheless, Immelt went on a $175 billion buying spree of companies, many of which were overpriced, had underperformed, or subsequently failed. Among them were subprime mortgage companies that expanded GE Credit immediately before the Great Recession. Otherwise, the most notable failures involved spending "billions buying into the energy and power markets at their peaks," capped by purchasing the power and grid business of the French company Alstom for $13.7 billion in 2015. Before the sale, Alstom's 2014 Annual Report had reported "excess capacity in developed markets." And perhaps predictably, the market for its gas turbines cratered after GE's purchase was finalized. [50] [51] [52]

The lessons from GE are more complicated than "Jack Welch is good," and "Jeff Immelt is bad." Many of Immelt's strategies were a continuation of Welch's work, including the focus on GE Credit and the relentless approach of growing the company through acquisitions. Further, the 2007 financial crisis was shocking to almost every industry and hit GE Credit—over half of the company's revenue—particularly hard. But ultimately, the responsibility for GE's post-Jack Welch decline does lie with Immelt, and the two eras serve as excellent examples of **succeeding or failing to use the principle of mass appropriately**.

Welch evaluated the company he took over and applied *mass* to making sweeping changes that boosted efficiency, improved leadership and employee performance, and cut loose underperforming assets. He also accurately assessed the *existing environment* and focused his "massed combat power" on expanding GE's credit business and undertaking a series of acquisitions of industry-leading companies. All of this achieved the objective: propelling GE to huge profits and growth.

Immelt largely continued this strategy, but here's the thing: ***it was unsustainable and no longer worked***. Whereas Welch had identified "the decisive place and time" to "concentrate the effects of combat power," Immelt failed half of that equation. The decisive place and time had changed, but GE's application of combat power did not. In military terms, the company was throwing its 'troops' into a headlong slaughter.

Remember, none of The Nine Principles of War work in isolation:

- **Surprise** and **security** played a role in GE's decline, as the unexpected collapse of the subprime mortgage market and the recession that followed hammered the company's primary source of revenue.

- Since Welch's strategy of never-ending growth through acquisitions may have run its course, it was likely time to revise GE's **objective**, and **maneuver** to strike at an advantageous place.

- In the final equation, Immelt's GE failed to apply **mass** at the decisive place and time.

The venerable corporate giant was dropped from the Dow Jones Industrial average in 2018—after a *110-year run* on the index of the world's most prestigious companies. [53]

In the broadest sense, consider how many successful companies position their resources to utilize the principle of mass. Amazon dominates online retail and several other digital sectors with a relentless focus on seamless distribution and customer experience. Whole Foods built a wildly successful brand around the provision of "quality food" and dominated the marketplace to the point that Amazon acquired the company and included it in its portfolio of winning companies. Rolex remains wholly dedicated to the luxury watch market and deploys its massed resources accordingly.

Again, this principle doesn't just apply to overall business strategy. Mass can govern how departments within companies deploy their resources, who they hire and how they put them to work, and even how individual leaders lead.

In every application, success requires making a conscious, well-informed decision about where and when the greatest opportunities or threats exist—and then throwing the weight of your forces against them in an intelligent and coordinated manner.

> *"To achieve victory we must mass our forces at the hub of all power and movement. The enemy's 'center of gravity.'"*
>
> —CARL VON CLAUSEWITZ

4

ECONOMY OF FORCE

*Allocate minimum essential combat power
to secondary efforts.*

Many entrepreneurs and businesses fall prey to "Shiny Object Syndrome." A new software platform holds the promise of revolutionizing operations or sales when the current one works great. A leader institutes new procedures based on a popular business self-help book, without evaluating whether the changes fit an existing culture. A stable, growing company chases "hyper-growth" by differentiating into products and services that stray from its core offerings, purpose, and expertise. [54]

Individual projects often suffer from "scope creep." An effort grows far beyond its original intent. New features, functions, and subprojects accrue because of a poorly defined objective, or silos of team members working without coordination. Budgets are blown out of the water, and the end product—if it ever exists—is far different than the original intent. [55]

Companies often strategically diversify to chase growth or for the sake of diversification itself, and stray too far off course. The results can be poor and even disastrous:

Northrop Grumman [was] the fourth largest defense contractor in 2010. It has always been successful with electronics and robotic systems, but in 2001 it diversified into shipbuilding for the Navy. While we can't exactly use a Titanic metaphor to describe this effort, we could probably use an anchor one. This venture was very expensive, had razor-thin margins, and did not sync with any of Northrop's other businesses. In March 2011, Northrop's CEO said they got out of the shipping business to avoid "a drag on its bottom line for years to come." [56]

These common business problems result from a lack of disciplined focus that violates a **Principle of War: Economy of force**.

Marshaling Resources and Staying Focused on the Objective

Consider a Marine Corps infantry platoon tasked with seizing an enemy outpost situated on a hill overlooking a valley. In two days, the main force will move through that valley—and it needs the outpost gone to achieve surprise and avoid taking casualties from an elevated enemy position. It is the infantry platoon's objective to seize the outpost and eliminate the threat in support of the broader objective.

On the way to the target, the platoon commander spots an enemy reconnaissance patrol. The enemy soldiers are outnumbered five to one and unaware of the attacking platoon's presence. With a little maneuver, the commander could move into position for a perfect ambush and wipe out that enemy patrol. It's a tempting target. The aggressive lieutenant instinctively itches to set up and attack—crushing victory seems like a sure thing. Instead, he reports the enemy contact and moves away toward his real objective: the outpost on the hill.

This hypothetical example is a simple illustration of **economy of force**. Attacking that patrol would throw off the operation's time-table. It could alert individuals at the enemy outpost to the platoon's presence or result in casualties that weaken the force during the attack on the true **objective**. No matter how attractive the target, a wise commander refrains from diluting his combat power on a "side project." And a wise leader above that platoon commander communicates that targets of opportunity which imperil the timely seizure of the objective aren't targets of opportunity at all.

Again, executing this Principle of War relies on the others. **Objective** is the prominent factor. But **economy of force** is also inextricably intertwined with **mass**—"concentrate the effects of combat power at the decisive place and time." Distractions and a dilution of resources limit your ability to hit hard where it really matters. Marine Corps officer training elaborates on the idea:

> This goes hand-in-hand with the concept of mass. In order for us to concentrate decisive combat power at the decisive point, we must know where to economize forces at our secondary efforts. This also implies an acceptance of calculated risk at these secondary efforts. Limited attacks, defense, deceptions, or delaying actions can help us economize forces allowing us to weight the main effort with mass. [57]

Military Examples of Economy of Force

An excellent real-world example of economy of force is found in the application of special operations forces (SOF) by the military. These units are specially trained to conduct a range of missions where using conventional forces would be unsuccessful or overkill.

Rescuing hostages typically calls for 1st Special Forces Operational Detachment-Delta (Delta Force) or the Naval Special Warfare Development Group (commonly referred to as Seal Team 6). Sensitive rescues and medical treatment of personnel need Air Force Special Tactics Pararescuemen (PJs). U.S. Army Green Berets specialize in training and marshaling indigenous forces who may serve as the main effort in a conflict or a vital force-multiplier of conventional forces. These highly specialized roles serve as a scalpel in situations where a hammer won't do.

Another example of the principle is the military's use of contractors during the recent wars in Iraq and Afghanistan. Though the practice is widely known for its controversies, the overall employment of contractors was born of necessity and strategic considerations. Precious U.S. military personnel and combat power were devoted to fighting insurgencies. At the same time, contractors handled the everyday logistics, from food to laundry service, and the protection of supply convoys and civilian government personnel.

A significant economy of force debate also rages over the overall strategies in the recent wars in Iraq and Afghanistan. If the primary objective is to disrupt or destroy overseas terrorist networks before they can execute attacks on the United States, many analysts criticize the strategy used. They argue that the use of intelligence services, special operations forces, and local security partners is a far more economical use of force than invasions followed by nation-building efforts. [58]

Business Examples of Economy of Force

The economic fallout from the COVID-19 pandemic pushed many companies out of business while forcing others to learn economy of force. Many organizations had to make staff cuts, conserve resources, and ensure sufficient cash flow to weather the crisis. Black swan events and routine economic recessions alike spur a close examination of **objective**, **defense**, **offensive**, **maneuver**, and other Principles of War. But **economy of force** and "Bang for the Buck" reign supreme.

Many organizations recognized and eliminated positions they did not need and found new ways to get tasks done more efficiently. The crisis caused many businesses to restructure their operations with greater efficiency and effectiveness. And regardless of an economic crisis, successful companies *always* keep this principle front and center.

Outsourcing is a good example of a business tactic that can help companies achieve economy of force in the execution of various operational functions and tasks. A small-to-mid-size company may not need a fully staffed IT department, a server room, or even individual operating systems for employees. IT is essential, but it's not a core business function. Thus, the company may outsource tech support to contractors, utilize the services of companies offering cloud-computing platforms, and implement virtual and remote business concepts and practices that reduce personnel, hardware, software, and other infrastructure costs dramatically while maintaining effectiveness.

A small business may need some marketing support—say, organizing and administering social media campaigns that requires perhaps 10 hours of actual work per week. Hiring a full-time employee would involve coming up with "make-work" tasks to fill the remaining 30 hours, along with the significant expense associated with health insurance, workers' compensation insurance, and other benefits, office space, and personal equipment normally provided to full-time employees. It is far more efficient to hire a freelance contractor to meet the need while saving financial resources for core activities, and investing in enabling technologies and tools that can make the company's 'front-line fighters" more effective and efficient as they perform revenue generating activities.

Many companies take this concept a step further with "offshoring"—moving some business processes overseas to leverage reduced payroll, tax, and other expenses. This effort could involve having a physical presence in another country, such as Ford's move to build electric cars in Mexico. The decision saved costs, and Ford claims that one of its U.S. factories "will get an even larger investment than previously planned and will focus on making a range of self-driving cars." Resources have been salvaged and redeployed toward a key objective. [59]

Then, there is divestiture, which often illustrates how the Principles of War work together. Many companies realize that certain lines of business or specific units are no longer aligned with their enterprise level **objectives**. **Economy of force** causes them to close, sell, or otherwise dispose of these business lines and sub-units. In turn, this enables them to more effectively **maneuver**—redirecting that combat power toward achieving **mass** on essential efforts or new, profitable opportunities.

Bain & Company Partners Michael Mankins and David Harding provide an example of an effective divestiture in the *Harvard Business Review*:

> [L]ook at the $16 billion forest-products company Weyerhaeuser. Since 2004, it has divested operations totaling more than $9 billion and used the capital raised and the management resources released to transform itself from a traditional pulp-and-paper company into a leader in timber, building materials, and real estate. In the process, Weyerhaeuser has produced some of the highest returns in its sector.

The authors also note:

> [A] Bain & Company study found in an analysis of 7,315 divestitures completed by 742 companies over a 20-year period:

An investment of $100 dollars in the average company in 1987 would have been worth roughly $1,000 at the end of 2007, but a similar investment made in a portfolio of the "best divestors" would have been worth more than $1,800. [60]

Applications of Economy of Force

Carefully evaluating risks, assessing the return on investment (ROI) of specific ventures is crucial to any company. Having done so, deciding where to place resources is an obvious next step. Applying the concept of Economy of Force—from top to bottom—will prevent inappropriate or unbalanced growth, where departments or entire companies can grow into bloated or top-heavy bureaucracies, resulting in a perpetual cash drain that detracts from the pursuit and attainment of more lucrative opportunities.

> *"I could lick those fellows any day, but it would cost me 10,000 men, and as this is the last army England has, we must take care of it."*
>
> —WELLINGTON

5

MANEUVER

Place the enemy in a disadvantageous position through
the flexible application of combat power.

In December 1940, 36,000 UK, Australian, and Free French soldiers faced off against 150,000 Italian troops at the small port town of Sidi Barrani in Egypt. In addition to their manpower advantage, the Italians enjoyed a more than 10-to-one superiority in guns and a roughly two-to-one position in aircraft and tanks.

Within four days, however, the allied forces under British command utterly routed their enemies. They took the port and its defenses and "captured 4 generals, 38,000 men, 237 guns and 73 tanks," while only losing 624 men. [61] [62]

How was this lopsided victory possible? Much like the German Army's stunning capture of France that same year, the allied victory at Sidi Barrani relied on **maneuver**.

British Major General Richard O'Connor "made maximum use of security by approaching at night and staggering departure times and dates. While conducting a diversionary attack on the coastal city of Maktila, his mechanized forces were passing through a gap in Graziani's defenses to attack other camps from the rear. ... The attacks were quick, unexpected and followed the unmined path that led into the rear of each camp." [63]

The battle plan's stealth, detailed coordination of artillery, armor, airpower, and infantry, and its quick maneuver to strike from an unexpected angle enabled the defeat of a numerically superior force. This battle, among many others, illustrates the immense power of the fifth Principle of War.

Maneuver: A Principle of War *and* a Warfare Doctrine

The US military studied the lessons from many of the famous battles of World War II, exemplified by the German "Blitzkrieg" ("Lightning War") campaigns, and integrated maneuver warfare into its official doctrine. In particular, the Marine Corps had oriented itself around the concept by the 1980s.

MCDP (Marine Corps Doctrinal Publication) 1: Warfighting describes its application:

> The Marine Corps concept for winning ... is a warfighting doctrine based on rapid, flexible, and opportunistic maneuver. ... The essence of maneuver is taking action to generate and exploit some kind of advantage over the enemy as a means of accomplishing our objectives as effectively as possible. ...
>
> Especially important is maneuver in time—we generate a faster operating tempo than the enemy to gain a temporal advantage. It is through maneuver in all dimensions that an inferior force can achieve decisive superiority at the necessary time and place. [64]

Maneuver warfare is essentially the modern, sophisticated version of the **maneuver Principle of War** that predates the famous examples of the 20th Century.

- Maneuver was used by General Robert E. Lee when he split his forces to achieve a lopsided victory at the Battle of Chancellorsville in 1863. The Army of Northern Virginia defeated 115,000 troops of the Army of the Potomac with just 60,000 men by striking the enemy's unprotected right flank. [65]

- At the Battle of Austerlitz, Napoleon Bonaparte withdrew a portion of his 68,000 troops to draw 90,000 Russian and Austrian forces into a trap. He had stealthily deployed the bulk of his men to the left as the enemy attacked to his right. Napoleon's left wing then conducted a surprise, massed attack on the allied center's right flank to rout the opposing army. [66] [67]

- In 216 BC, the Carthaginian General Hannibal ordered his 50,000-strong force to conduct a double envelopment, also known as a "pincer movement," to destroy a Roman army of roughly 80,000 men. "Roman losses [ranged] from 55,000 (according to Roman historian Livy) to 70,000 (according to Greek historian Polybius)," whereas "the Carthaginians lost about 6,000 men." [68]

These examples show the incredible value of maneuvering to strike at precisely the right place—at exactly the right time.

Maneuver Relies on Identifying Problems and Opportunities, Followed by a Fast, Flexible Reaction

Business leaders aren't crushing enemies on a literal battlefield, of course. But the principle of maneuver certainly applies in non-military contexts. And as the Marine Corps explains when training new officers, it works in concert with the other Principles of War:

> Maneuver alone will not defeat a force, however maneuver in conjunction with Mass, Surprise, and Economy of Force allows a seemingly inferior force to achieve decisive superiority at the necessary time and place. [69]

Let's say you have a well-defined, achievable **objective**. You have **massed** your resources to where they will do the most good, while minimizing resources for secondary efforts to fulfill **economy of force**. When does **maneuver** come into the picture? It's needed when there is an opportunity or a challenge.

Perhaps a competitor starts moving in on your territory, and you must adjust to counter the threat and fulfill the principle of **security**. Often, maneuver is called for when someone spots a novel opportunity to advance the objective.

This could be a new marketing campaign, a diversion of manpower toward a quickly devised project, or an agile expansion of services that meet a pressing market need. As long as the new effort supports the objective—and the objective remains viable in changing circumstances—maneuver is a good idea.

The keys to applying this principle are:

1. The ability to quickly and accurately identify a problem or opportunity

2. The ability to react intelligently and rapidly, while retaining flexibility to adapt to changing situations

Both of these qualities rely on another concept that's used by the best military and business organizations: decentralized command. While most people think of the military as a rigid, hierarchical organization, its leadership schools teach, and quality units have a high degree of, flexibility and initiative. As I shared before, these qualities are mentioned on my book, *Trust-Based Leadership*, and are a pivotal consideration when utilizing delegation and, once again, the indispensable concept of "commander's intent."

The commander's intent clearly explains the objective that must be accomplished through "mission-type orders." Consider the following order: "Secure the Dong Ha bridge in order to prevent enemy forces from seizing, controlling or crossing it. The intent is to protect the left flank of our main force."

Specific tasks required to achieve this objective are delegated to lower-level leaders who work out the details of how to fulfill the intent. These leaders have the latitude to take the initiative and adapt, especially when faced with novel opportunities or problems. To continue our bridge example, if a platoon leader arrives at the bridge and sees excellent defensive high ground beyond it, he may move his platoon forward and set up on a hill. He is achieving the commander's intent (protecting the flank of the main force) as well as the objective (the bridge is secured).

Why is this relevant to maneuver? In all but the smallest organizations, senior leadership may be far removed from the problems and opportunities that arise on the "front lines." Thus, the only way to effectively maneuver is to empower trusted leaders at all levels to react and seize the initiative. As organizations grow larger, this flexible leadership framework becomes exponentially more valuable.

Maneuver Warfare in Business and Politics

President Barack Obama is often dubbed "the first social-media president." His administration employed a team of 20 headed by a former Twitter executive to create posts, memes, videos, and graphics that established his personal brand and supported his policies and initiatives. [70] [71]

As Kevin Freking wrote for the Associated Press in 2017:

> The year Obama came into office, the White House joined Facebook, Twitter, Flickr, Vimeo, iTunes and MySpace. In 2013, the first lady posted her first photo to Instagram. In 2015, the president sent his first tweet from @POTUS, an account that now has 11 million followers. [In 2017], the White House posted its first official story on Snapchat, a promotion of the president's State of the Union address. [72]

The Obama administration's embrace of social media was merely a continuation of the campaign's revolutionary use of it during the 2008 and 2012 elections. This strategy achieved its full potential during the latter effort, when the campaign used a combination of memes, Big Data collection and application, and carefully crafted messaging to significant effect:

> Obama dominated the social media space because his team got how networks work. The real power of social media is not in the number of posts or Tweets but in user engagement measured by content spreadability. For example, Obama logged twice as many Facebook "Likes" and nearly 20 times as many re-tweets as Romney. With his existing social media base and spreadable content, Obama had far superior reach. [73]

Obama's campaigns and administration recognized an opportunity—the splintering of traditional media and the rise of social networks—and maneuvered to win the medium.

Netflix is another good example of this principle. Starting as a mail-order DVD service in 1997, the company leveraged the growing power of the internet while making a series of dramatic pivots to become the entertainment juggernaut it is today. "For Netflix ... doing the obvious rarely meant taking the easy way out. It meant making business decisions that were so difficult and so ambitious, few people could even see them, let alone understand them." [74]

The company first unveiled a mail-order subscription model with no late fees and return dates. It then pioneered the use of algorithms to recommend media to customers, quickly shifted from rentals to online streaming as technology evolved. And it eventually reinvented itself as a TV and movie studio to generate original content that customers crave. Netflix's latest model is something that competing services emulate and see as a necessity to compete in streaming services. [75]

Southwest Airlines is a great example of maneuvering to succeed in an industry that routinely struggles to maintain profitability:

> Southwest Airlines' business model is based on extremely efficient operations, low-cost pricing, and innovative logistics solutions. Furthermore, their strategy also includes a deep focus on customer experience and looking ahead. Finally, none of this would be possible without a motivated team of employees. Through this sound strategy, Southwest achieved multiple competitive advantages that have allowed it to stay relevant in a rapidly changing world.[76]

Among all of its advantages, the airline's focus on hiring the right people and training them to provide a better customer experience is perhaps the most important. While lousy food, travel delays, and poor customer service are hallmarks of the industry, Southwest has found a way to keep costs low *and* please its passengers. The airline achieved the top customer service score in JD Power's latest travel survey—a position it has routinely held over the years. [77] [78]

Maneuver is the Flexible Application of "Combat Power"

As with every Principle of War, maneuver applies in organizational and personal ways. Enterprises must swiftly pivot to capitalize on opportunities and meet challenges, as must departments, projects, and individual leaders. Quickly implementing a new, more efficient distribution system or a less-expensive supplier require flexibility, as does a leader's decision to reorganize her time or hire individuals to work on new projects.

In every situation, applying the principle effectively relies on quickly identifying a problem or opportunity, followed by reacting rapidly. Nimble people and organizations that maneuver effectively run circles around those that are stuck in place.

"Move not unless you see an advantage; use not your troops unless there is something to be gained; fight not unless the position is critical."

—SUN TZU, *THE ART OF WAR*

6

UNITY OF COMMAND

*For every objective, ensure unity of effort
under one responsible commander.*

Operation Eagle Claw was a daring 1980 mission to rescue 52 Americans held hostage by radical students at the U.S. embassy in Tehran, Iran. It was also a tactical failure that had grave strategic and geopolitical implications. In hindsight, from the very start of the planning for this mission, the leaders allowed planners to ignore an essential Principle of War: Unity of Command.

The plan was incredibly complicated. It marshaled various ground, air, and naval assets and relied on perfect planning and coordination between each branch of the U.S. military and various federal agencies, all while maintaining strict operational security (OPSEC).

Navy helicopters flown by Marine Corps pilots launched from a Navy aircraft carrier and traveled to a patch of Iranian desert called "Desert One." Air Force C-130 cargo planes carried U.S. Army Delta Force operators and Rangers from Oman to this landing zone, where they staged for the rescue. The men were to be helicoptered to just outside the Iranian capital. Then, they would move toward the embassy in vehicles, conduct the rescue, and evacuate by helicopter from a nearby stadium. The evacuation helicopters planned to refuel at a separate airbase that had been captured by another unit of Army Rangers who had been transported there by the Air Force.

When the mission began, problems accrued quickly. Two of the eight helicopters aborted—one due to mechanical issues and the other because of a dust storm. A third helicopter that safely landed at Desert One suffered a hydraulic failure. Commanders on the ground debated whether to proceed. But with only five working helos on a mission that called for at least six, the operation was called off.

As everyone prepared to depart the landing zone, disaster struck. A helicopter pilot lost his reference point in the dust kicked up by rotor wash and crashed into a C-130 tanker. Eight pilots and crewmen were killed, and several others injured in the explosion and fire. The remaining personnel boarded the rest of the planes and retreated. Five helicopters, numerous classified documents, and the bodies of the dead were left behind and captured by the Iranians. [79] [80]

The disastrous operation made international news and significantly damaged American prestige. Operation Eagle Claw also highlighted organizational problems in the U.S. military and burgeoning special operations community. And it dramatically changed how joint operations worked in the future.

An investigation commissioned by the U.S. Joint Chiefs of Staff determined that the rescue's planning was "ad hoc" and suffered from significant command and control issues. Four service branches had to coordinate for the complex operations to work. And each of the different elements—the helicopter pilots, the C-130 pilots, the ships, and the assaulters—had individual leaders, some of whom didn't see eye to eye. [81] [82] [83]

The plan's execution relied on a great deal of *cooperation* rather than *control* under one clearly defined leader. The Joint Chiefs' investigation spurred the Goldwater Nichols DOD Reorganization Act of 1986, which improved the military's coordination of service branches. The U.S. Special Operations Command (USSOCOM) was also formed to oversee all special operations forces. [84]

The relatively smooth joint operations we see today are a direct result of these changes. And perhaps the primary lesson the military relearned from the Desert One debacle is the need for **unity of command**.

Well-Defined Leadership Enables Consistent, Coordinated Execution

As detailed in the last chapter, agile organizations empower leaders at all levels to use initiative while accomplishing a mission. Mission-type orders have a clear objective and state the commander's intent. As long as the subordinate leader's actions fulfill this intent, he or she can issue innovative orders that accomplish the task.

Despite this latitude, **a single leader is still responsible for each unit and sets a clear commander's intent**. This individual must align their intent with the higher-level objective and coordinate units. Just about everything depends on this well-defined structure, as described in Marine Corps officer training:

> Mass, economy of force, and maneuver would be impossible without the vision of a single leader. To ensure that vision is carried to the lowest levels while still allowing for flexibility and initiative we use commander's intent. It allows for and leverages mass, objective, and economy of force at the decisive point. [85]

This relationship between unity of command, the other Principles of War, and commander's intent is crucial. The best organizations, business or military, are decentralized but delegate within a coherent leadership structure. Empowering leaders at different levels to adapt—*within the direction of the intent*—creates organizations that relentlessly move toward their objectives while also being fast and flexible.

This structure does involve unique requirements and potential challenges. Militaries and businesses must heavily invest in leadership selection and development because each leader must be competent and trusted. The negative impact of poor leadership increases as you move up the chain. Higher-level commanders must deal with increasingly complex coordination and ensure that their intent matches up with the strategic objectives.

This issue is addressed by hiring, training, and promoting the best leaders, as well as through supervision, responsibility, and accountability. A general or top executive has to delegate many things, but he or she is responsible for all of them and should be held accountable when they fail. Leaders must ensure the successful execution of orders through supervision. You may not be completing all of the assigned tasks yourself, but you need to supervise them adequately to make sure they are accomplished. In *Trust-Based Leadership*, I call <u>supervision</u> a leader's *"secret weapon."*

Trust-Based Leadership™ with Effective Unity of Command

The opposite of a decentralized structure—a single leader who makes all of the detailed decisions—has more significant weaknesses. In these settings, success or failure resides in the competence of one individual who makes or breaks an organization. And given the complexity of modern business and military operations, it's simply impossible for one person (or a handful of people) to have the visibility and mental bandwidth to make all front-line decisions.

The best companies, departments, militaries, and units invest in good leaders and implement what I've termed "Trust-Based Leadership™." Delegating mission-type orders with a clear commander's intent **under a united command** meets objectives faster and better.

There are varying degrees of decentralization that take place under a well-defined chain of command. Some businesses set relatively rigid overall, departmental, and unit objectives, while still allowing front-line employees latitude while accomplishing these goals. Others practice something resembling laissez-faire (hands-off) management, while still maintaining the principle of Unity of Command. A good example of the latter scenario is Warren Buffet's multinational conglomerate, Berkshire Hathaway.

Berkshire Hathaway has enjoyed tremendous success through a strategy of acquiring quality companies, instituting a common culture, and setting well-defined financial objectives. It provides these acquisitions with additional resources but allows them to essentially function as they always have. A good way to describe this model is "if it ain't broke, don't fix it."

Nevertheless, the holding company still implements a strong culture, sets clear objectives and intent, and holds these companies accountable, thus maintaining the unity of command. The management style may be hands-off—but the leadership's authority is very clear. And the results of this model are inarguable. [86] [87]

Buffet took control of Berkshire Hathaway—then, a textile manufacturing firm—in 1965, and morphed it into an insurance and investment company. Over the following decades, he acquired numerous companies in incredibly diverse sectors, but always focused on those with "stable, almost predictable long-term growth." Between 1965 and 2006, the company's shareholders averaged 21% yearly returns. Berkshire Hathaway is also now the 12th biggest company in the world, even though it only has 25 employees working at its Omaha, NE headquarters. [88] [89]

The Berkshire Hathaway example is notable because it illustrates that **unity of command does not necessarily mean rigid command.** Yes, the lines of authority flowing down an org chart are rigid, but all decisions and execution certainly don't need to be.

All models, from laissez-faire decentralization to authoritarian leadership, benefit from knowing exactly who has authority—and who is setting the strategy and direction.

Unity of Command Failures

The consequences of violating this principle are increased conflict, ineffective execution, missed opportunities, unresolved issues, and inefficiency.

In 2019, the multinational software company SAP SE appointed two CEOs after Bill McDermott stepped down. Former COO Christian Klein ran things at SAP's headquarters in Walldorf, Germany, while Jennifer Morgan, former president of the Cloud Business Group, focused on the company's American operations.

"As they have already demonstrated, Jennifer and Christian complement each other perfectly and will be strong co-CEOs, a leadership model that is time-tested at SAP with multiple prior instances of success," said Professor Hasso Plattner, chairman of the Supervisory Board of SAP SE. [90] [91]

Six months later, however, Morgan was out. "More than ever, the current environment requires companies to take swift, determined action which is best supported by a very clear leadership structure," the company said in a statement. [92]

SAP SE became the third software company to abandon a dual-CEO model in the past year, joining Oracle and Salesforce. Charles Elson, the director of the John L. Weinberg Center for Corporate Governance at the University of Delaware, commented on the move in Bloomberg: "Two heads are not better than one. When you have two CEOs, there are inevitable clashes between the two. One will dominate and the other has to go. They always end up with one person being CEO." [93]

Weak unity of command also often results from acquisitions and mergers. One of the biggest corporate failures in history happened when AOL bought Time-Warner for $160 billion in 2001. The deal—designed to leverage each company's dominance in traditional and internet media—was the biggest merger to date. But along with problems caused by the bursting dot-com bubble, AOL Time Warner suffered conflict between leaders. In particular, "the politicized and turf-protecting culture of Time Warner made realizing anticipated synergies that much more difficult." [94]

Eventually, the company removed AOL from its name, and Time Warner proceeded to spin off, sell, or split its numerous assets over the next 17 years. By 2018, "none of the sprawling businesses that made up AOL Time Warner [stood] as a separate publicly traded company." [95]

These examples and many more illustrate why successful companies, departments, and projects depend on clear leadership that flows from a single point. A unified command enables clear direction, coordinates subordinate units, directs resources appropriately, and avoids inevitable conflict when multiple parties have equal authority.

While objective is the Principle of War from which all other principles flow, unity of command is the glue that holds them together.

> *"An army should have but one chief;*
> *a greater number is detrimental."*
>
> —Niccolo Machiavelli

7

SECURITY

*Never permit the enemy to acquire
an unexpected advantage.*

Ideal military operations relentlessly pursue the **offensive** and **maneuver** to meet challenges and seize opportunities. Commanders **mass** combat power at the pivotal point and use **economy of force** to minimize resources devoted toward secondary objectives. These Principles of War rightly focus on staying offensive. But, as an often-used military saying goes, "the enemy gets a vote."

A leader has a core duty to prepare for threats and implement sufficient **security**. Failing to do so imperils the other principles and, fundamentally, the successful attainment of the **objective**.

The Lebanese Civil War, which raged from 1975 to 1990, was a complex multi-sectarian conflict. It started when "the Phalangists, a Christian militia, clashed with Palestinian factions over the latter's armed struggle against Israel from Lebanese territory." But the war soon devolved into a complicated struggle for the future of the Lebanese state, with numerous local, regional, and international forces entering the fray. There were more than 20 belligerents, including various militias, the Lebanese Army, and foreign nations. [96]

To describe this conflict as a "complicated threat environment" is an understatement.

The U.S. military became involved in 1982 when the Reagan Administration feared that fighting between Israel and Syria might escalate to a wider Arab-Israeli war. A force of 800 U.S. Marines arrived in August as part of a multinational peacekeeping force. The initial mission was "to protect Palestinian civilians" and oversee the withdrawal of the Palestinian Liberation Organization (PLO). But the subsequent assassination of the Israeli-backed Lebanese prime minister sparked a new crisis and another invasion by Israel. The multinational force's mission soon became ensuring the withdrawal of all foreign troops from Lebanon and empowering the Lebanese Army. [97] [98]

Many Lebanese citizens welcomed the peacekeepers, but they soon became targets for terrorists and militias. On April 18, 1983, a car bomb exploded at the U.S. embassy in Beirut and killed 63 people, including 17 Americans. In the months that followed, militias shelled the Marines stationed near Beirut International Airport with mortars, rockets, and artillery, and there were many instances of pitched firefights between the Marines and local Muslim militias. And on October 23, a 19-ton truck filled with explosives detonated in the ground-level parking garage located under the building being used as the headquarters for the 1st Battalion, 8Th Marines.

> Marine sentries initially paid little attention to the Mercedes truck. Heavy vehicles were a common sight at the airport, and in fact the BLT was expecting one that day with a water delivery. The truck circled the parking lot, then picked up speed as it traveled parallel to a line of concertina wire protecting the south end of the Marine compound. Suddenly, the vehicle veered left, plowed through the 5-foot-high wire barrier and rumbled between two guard posts.
>
> By then it was obvious the driver of the truck—a bearded man with black hair—had hostile intentions, but there was no way to stop him. [99]

Despite the previous vehicle-borne suicide bombing and other attacks, and intelligence reports that additional attacks against US forces were being planned, security to the Marine headquarters remained incredibly lax. And terrorists from Hezbollah, Iran, and Syria's proxy, exploited this "unexpected advantage" to organize and execute the bombing. In its aftermath, the Department of Defense commissioned an independent investigation that found security "neither commensurate with the increasing level of threat ... nor sufficient to preclude catastrophic losses." [100]

Less than four months later, President Ronald Reagan ended U.S. involvement in the peacekeeping mission. Imad Mughniyah, the Hezbollah terrorist who planned the bombing, was indicted by a U.S. grand jury two years after the attack but remained free for another 25 years. Mughniyah was killed by a car bomb in 2008, an assassination reported to have been a joint CIA-Mossad operation. [101] [102]

The Beirut bombing is a powerful example of the consequences of failing to implement the principle of Security. The tragedy involved the highest single day loss of life suffered by the Marine Corps since Vietnam, and it caused the U.S. mission's essential failure. It is far from the only example of security failures, however. The 2001 terrorist attacks on the World Trade Center and the Pentagon took place despite al Qaeda declaring war on the U.S. in 1996, and the fact that a less spectacular bombing attack hit the World Trade Center in 1993. [103] [104]

Good Security Enables Offense

The principle of security is not intended to completely shield an organization from risk or harm. Taken to an extreme, it would prevent a military unit or business from aggressively pursuing the objective. Instead, this principle involves vigilant analysis and awareness of potential threats, along with contingency plans and quick measures to deal with them.

Marine Corps officer training emphasizes maintaining the upper hand against opponents:

> We look to, at appropriate times and places, adopt measures to prevent the enemy from imposing their will on us faster than we can react. It allows us to ensure our freedom of action on the battlefield and preserve our combat power for decisive action. It does not imply the over-application of caution to eliminate risk, but rather seeks to enhance our operations through bold maneuver and acceptance of calculated risk. [105]

In business, "the enemy" takes a variety of forms. It could be a direct competitor who eats into your company's market share by undercutting pricing. An enemy might be a natural disaster, a supply chain disruption, a class-action lawsuit, or a "black swan event," such as the COVID-19 pandemic. Threats can be self-imposed, such as when executives "bet the farm" on an initiative that represents a single point of failure for the company. And quite often, enemies are the disruptors that change an entire industry that never saw them coming.

A Disruptor That Must Look to Its Own Defense

Peloton has made an enormous splash in the fitness industry, merging sales of equipment—stationary bikes that cost over $2,000—with a recurring revenue model based on a paid subscription to virtual exercise classes. The company has taken market share from a range of companies in the fitness industry, from home equipment seller NordicTrack to commercial gyms, to exercise class purveyors, like SoulCycle.

In 2014, the company was founded on the premise of making in-person cycling classes more convenient by taking them into the home. The development of original content—a large number of exercise classes and a competitive scoreboard among subscribers—has developed a committed, loyal customer base that evangelizes for the brand.

> According to Peloton's IPO prospectus, the company had 511,000 connected-fitness subscribers in late 2019 and a 95 percent retention rate. It has sold more than 550,000 machines—a number that includes its bike and its treadmill, the Tread. The most popular on-demand classes have tens of thousands of rides completed; special live rides have been known to pull in nearly 20,000 live riders at one time. [106]

The question for Peloton's competitors is, "did they see this coming?" Regardless, when the threat to their market share was recognized, how did they react, and how quickly? As of early 2020, Peloton had a market cap of over $13 billion, "more than double the market value of Planet Fitness, which is the most popular low-cost fitness center chain in the U.S." Planet Fitness, along with other gyms, is under severe financial threat from the COVID-19 lockdowns as of this writing, with both 24-Hour Fitness and Gold's Gym filing for bankruptcy in the first half of 2020. [107] [108]

Peloton's success has gained it some direct competitors, including efforts by venerable exercise equipment makers. Icon Health & Fitness, which owns NordicTrack, ProForm, and other brands, has the iFit streaming fitness platform, which raised $200 million in equity to develop content and boasted about 330,000 members in late 2019. Other competitors, such as Tonal, Mirror, and Echelon Fit—the latter offering a much cheaper exercise bike—are also crowding into the space. Thus, while Peloton disrupted fitness competitors, now the company needs to consider its security and how to react to these challenges. [109]

The economic fallout from COVID-19 has driven home the need for security. Though some experts had warned about the potential for a worldwide pandemic over the years, almost no one predicted this crisis and the impact of lockdowns. That said, many analysts had projected that a recession was on the horizon, and the quick bankruptcies and pleas for bailouts show that numerous industries weren't prepared for a major economic downturn.

Perhaps the most egregious examples are the airlines:

> [D]espite a history of rough patches during unforeseen events, such as the September 11, 2001, attacks and the volcanic eruption in Iceland in 2010 that disrupted air travel, large U.S. airline companies spent most of their free cash flow over the past 10 years on share buybacks, propping up their quarterly earnings-per-share results. [110]

The airline industry received government support after the crisis and expects to get additional bailouts because of air travel's vital role in the economy. But many politicians and taxpayers are understandably hostile to the idea of propping up an industry that routinely suffers bankruptcies or requires bailouts while failing to build cash reserves. [111]

It may be impossible to set security for a *specific* unforeseen disaster, but it's certainly possible to prepare for an event that will ground flights. And a basic contingency plan involves setting cash aside to weather the next economic storm.

Preparing for Threats Enables Offense

Again, adequate security supports the other Principles of War, and defensive planning and posture should never become prominent enough to slow or stop an organization from moving offensively. The basics of good security involve identifying potential threats such as moves by competitors, financial weaknesses, economic issues, lawsuits, data breaches, and regulatory changes that pose significant risks.

Once these threats are identified, leaders must develop contingency plans and assign sufficient resources to deal with the problem. These assets—such as a rainy-day fund or specific human resources—may be held in reserve and tapped when a bad situation arises. But first, they must exist, and contingency plans must outline what they are and how they will be used.

Stay vigilant for threats. Never gamble the organization's future on a long shot. And be prepared to fend off attacks from competitors and events that will imperil the company and its objective.

"When invading an enemy's country, men should always be confident in spirit, but they should fear too, and take measures of precaution; and thus they will beat once valorous in attack and impregnable in defense."

—ARCHIDAMUS OF SPARTA

8

SURPRISE

Strike the enemy at a time or place or in a manner
for which he is unprepared.

Military theorists regard surprise as one of the most potent advantages a combatant can possess, often eclipsing an overwhelming superiority in mass. Surprise increases the odds of a successful attack, reduces casualties for the attacker, and serves as a force multiplier, enabling weaker forces to defeat numerically and technologically dominant opponents.

Michael Handel, the former Professor of Naval Strategy at the U.S. Naval War College, described the advantages of surprise in *The Journal of Strategic Studies*:

> A successful unanticipated attack will facilitate the destruction of a sizable portion of the enemy's forces at a lower cost to the attacker by throwing the inherently stronger defense psychologically off balance, and hence temporarily reducing his resistance. [112]

This is a crucial observation on how **surprise** works and interacts with the other Principles of War: it takes away the enemy's agency. Opponents can't **mass** against a force they can't see, **maneuver** in light of an attack they don't know is coming, or set **security** to guard against the unknown. When a surprise attack is made effectively, the impact can be enormous—in war and in business.

Surprise Attacks that Succeed, and Others That Actually Fail

Possibly the most successful surprise attack in history, and the largest ambush, happened in 217 B.C. The Carthaginian general Hannibal Barca was menacing Rome and moved his forces between a Roman army sent to destroy him and their capital city. Hannibal goaded the Romans under General Gaius Flaminius into chasing him by burning the countryside. As the Carthaginians were being pursued south, they suddenly turned east along the shore of Lake Trasimene just before nightfall.

Hannibal moved his army through a pass bordered by the lake's shoreline on the south and forested hills on the north, camping once they reached the eastern edge of the pass. He made ready for battle the next day, and the Roman general entered the gorge the next morning ready to obliterate him. What Flaminius didn't know, however, was that Hannibal had hidden cavalry and infantry in the wooded hills above the lake the night before. After the Romans moved into the defile and made contact with the Carthaginians to their front, the bulk of Hannibal's forces swarmed down on the Romans from their secret positions.

The results were stunningly lopsided. Of 30,000 Roman soldiers, about half were killed, and the other half taken captive. The Carthaginians only lost about 1,500 men. [113]

General George Washington employed surprise a bit differently during the Christmas of 1776. The rebel army had suffered a series of recent setbacks, including being driven from their base of New York City in August and losing Fort Washington and Fort Lee in rapid succession in November. The rebel soldiers and their political supporters were demoralized, and potential foreign allies hesitated to get involved with a losing rebellion. Washington had to do something. [114]

Over the night and early morning of Dec. 25-26, Washington ordered 5,000 troops into boats to cross the Delaware River at three points. The weather was abominable; snow and sleet pelted the soldiers, and only Washington's main force of 2,400 made it across, hours late. The next morning, Washington split his troops into two columns and attacked a 1,500-man Hessian garrison at Trenton from the north and west. The surprise on the sleeping defenders was complete, and the victory was total. The Continental Army killed 20 Hessians, wounded about 80, and captured 900, compared to only five wounded Americans. [115] [116]

Both the Battles of Trasimene and Trenton relied on effective surprise, but their impacts were far different. At Trasimene, Hannibal utterly crushed the opposing army, effectively ending Roman resistance in the open field and fundamentally changing Roman strategy to "avoiding direct engagement [with Carthaginian forces] whenever possible." [117]

Washington's gains at Trenton were far more modest; it was a small battle against a small force, and the weight of the British Army was still intent on destroying his Continental Army. But it also accomplished a strategic objective:

> Washington's decision … was based on strategic motivation, understanding that the Continental Army desperately needed a victory after months of intense fighting with several significant defeats and no major victories. Washington also understood that the element of surprise was the only way that he and his army stood a chance of defeating the highly trained Hessian mercenaries. [118]

There are also examples of surprise attacks that seemed to work but ultimately failed, and they provide cautionary lessons. In December 1944, the German Army achieved complete surprise during its Ardennes Counteroffensive, commonly known as the Battle of the Bulge.

> Allied forces in the Ardennes consisted primarily of American troops—some new and inexperienced, others exhausted and battle-worn. The Germans had some initial success. They achieved complete surprise and pushed westwards through the middle of the American line, creating the 'bulge' that gave the battle its name. But this success was short-lived. [119]

A stubborn defense by the U.S. 101st Airborne Division at the vital chokepoint of Bastogne, Allied air superiority, stretched German supply lines, and the eventual relief of the defenders turned the largest battle fought on the Western Front into a resounding German defeat. [120]

Similarly, the Japanese Navy's attack at Pearl Harbor in 1941 was a shocking surprise and an initial victory—but one that presaged ultimate defeat. Because the Japanese Navy failed to catch U.S. aircraft carriers in port and destroy them, American forces could subsequently oppose the Japanese at the Battles of the Coral Sea and Midway.

Coral Sea was essentially fought to a draw but represented a strategic victory for the Allies, who prevented Japanese expansion that would have isolated and threatened Australia. It also marked the first time the Japanese had been stopped after a relentless string of victories. The Battle of Midway was even more significant. The remaining three carriers of the U.S. Pacific fleet surprised the Japanese as they attacked Midway Island. All four Japanese carriers were sunk to the loss of only one U.S. carrier—an outcome that fundamentally shifted the balance of naval power in the Pacific war. [121] [122]

The lesson from these battles and many others is that the principle of **surprise is most effectively employed in concert with the other Principles of War.** Just because you *can* conduct a successful surprise attack doesn't necessarily mean you *should*. In war and business, the principle of surprise must always help achieve the objective. And you must have enough resources, mass, and flexibility to capitalize on the advantage conferred by surprise.

Business Examples of Surprise

Amazon rolls out AWS

In the early 2000s, Cloud computing was a nascent application and industry, with various companies exploring platforms. At the time, Amazon was "simply an e-commerce company struggling with scale problems. Those issues forced the company to build some solid internal systems to deal with the hyper growth it was experiencing."

During an executive retreat in 2003, the Amazon team "realized they had also become quite good at running infrastructure services like compute, storage and database ... What's more, they had become highly skilled at running reliable, scalable, cost-effective data centers out of need." [123]

Three years later, Amazon launched Elastic Compute Cloud (Amazon EC2), "a web service that provides resizable compute capacity in the cloud." It was the first significant cloud solution to market, enabling the company to dominate the space. And despite substantial challenges from rivals like Google, IBM, and Microsoft, Amazon has never looked back from its perch as the cloud services leader. [124]

Of a $266 billion market in 2020, Amazon owns about a third of it (32.4%), and the company pulled in just over $35 billion in revenue in 2019. It's closest competitor is Microsoft, whose Azure platform accounts for only 17.6% of the market. [125] [126] [127]

The e-commerce giant had identified a core competency, developed it into a business that offered scalable, affordable cloud computing services, and surprised competitors with an immensely successful rollout and subsequent campaign. Today, "Amazon's Web-services division powers vast portions of the Internet, from Netflix to the C.I.A." [128]

Disney buys Pixar

Long known as the king of animated films, Walt Disney Animation was in bad shape in the early 2000s. "That's largely thanks to a series of 'expensive failures' like the 2D animated Hercules and the computer animated Chicken Little. And while movies like Mulan and Lilo & Stitch were considered to be better, their success with critics and at the box office was nothing compared to Disney's success in their animated renaissance of the 1990s." [129]

In 2006, Disney pulled a surprise move and acquired Pixar Animation, recognized as "Hollywood's most successful and acclaimed animation studio," for $7.4 billion. This industry-shaking decision turned out to be a great one. Of the $14 billion that Pixar made between 1995 and 2019, $11 billion happened after the Disney acquisition.

Beyond the financial rewards, the Disney-Pixar alliance has set the gold standard in animated content. Pixar films have earned seven Academy Awards since the merger, and the move even reinvigorated Disney Animation, which the company briefly considered shuttering after buying Pixar. Disney's animation properties now play a significant role in the company's overall box office dominance. Disney movies accounted for "38% of the total U.S. box office" in 2019, a number that was about 10% in 2006. [130] [131]

Surprise Is Immensely Effective—But It Requires Strategy

Again, surprise attacks are very powerful and confer tremendous and some-times insurmountable advantages. But they must be appropriately deployed to support the objective. Surprise also doesn't need to be complete to be effective, as Marine Corps officer training explains:

> It does not require the enemy to be caught unaware, but rath-er that he becomes aware too late to react effectively. May include the use of speed (maneuver in time), unexpected forc-es (mass), operating at night (psychological and technological maneuver), deception (psychological maneuver), security, variation in techniques, and use of unfavorable terrain (spatial maneuver). [132]

In business, a competitor may see certain moves coming but remain unable to marshal a response. A new product will be apparent to a competitor once it is rolled out or even in the testing phases. However, offering a similar product requires development, production, distribution, and more. When a company gets to market first, it has an opportunity to acquire an insurmountable ad-vantage over its competitors.

Whether this Principle of War is applied to a new product or service, a "sto-len" supplier, or a hostile takeover, the shocking move must make sense. The essential criteria for a successful surprise attack are:

- Does an opportunity exist, and is it significant enough to employ maneuver?

- Is it truly possible to achieve a surprise?

- Do you have the resources to take a surprise attack to its necessary conclusion—one that achieves or supports the objective?

When these questions are answered with a "yes," it is often time to strike hard and fast—and shock the competition.

"The execution of military surprise is always dangerous,
and the general who is never taken off his guard himself,
and never loses an opportunity of striking at an unguarded foe,
will be most likely to succeed in war."

—THUCYDIDES

9

SIMPLICITY

*Prepare clear, uncomplicated plans and clear, concise orders
to ensure thorough understanding.*

L ike many of the Principles of War, there are civilian versions of simplicity. The K.I.S.S. principle—"Keep it Simple, Stupid"—is widely used in business. But even that maxim has military origins.

K.I.S.S. is often attributed to Kelly Johnson, the former lead engineer of Lockheed's famous Skunk Works (Advanced Development Programs (A.D.P.)) department, which has designed military aircraft since 1943. It's also sometimes attributed to Rear Admiral Paul D. Stroop, Chief of the Bureau of Naval Weapons. In 1960, Stroop "instituted Project KISS to increase the reliability and reduce the cost of the military gadgets his organization produces." [133] [134] [135]

Whatever the exact origin, the K.I.S.S. principle has taken root as a mantra in product design, programming, and business—for a good reason. Simplicity is an essential virtue in complicated environments.

Simple, straightforward objectives, plans, directives and communications help ensure effective execution, better controlling the human element in chaotic and complex settings. This is why simplicity has particular value in combat. But it also has merits in business, especially within modern organizations and operating environments that grow more complicated every year.

Simplicity reduces internal friction

The Marine Corps teaches new officers the value of simplicity as an effective tool for reducing "friction:"

> Plans and orders should be as simple and direct as the situation and mission dictate. This reduces the chance of misunderstandings that inject internal friction and therefore cause ineffective execution. Ceteris paribus (all variables being equal), the simplest plan is preferred. [136]

Military friction is a term coined by the famed Prussian general and military strategist Carl von Clausewitz. He used it to describe all of the random elements that differentiate "real war" from "war on paper." Friction can include everything from supply issues, to lousy weather, to human failures.

"Everything in war is simple, but the simplest thing is difficult," Clausewitz wrote. "The difficulties accumulate and end by producing a kind of friction that is inconceivable unless one has experienced war." [137]

War's friction may be unique, but this concept is alive and well in business and many other organizational environments. There are two types of it:

- **External friction:** Challenges that arise outside of the organization, such as bad weather during a military campaign, or a hurricane that destroys a business's principal supplier. Leaders often have little control over external friction, though they can prepare contingency plans and reactions to these events.

- **Internal friction:** These problems come from within the organization, such as personality conflicts, the sudden loss of a vital employee, or bad leadership. Leaders have far more control over these issues—they can design a resilient organization that mitigates or avoids internal challenges.

Simplicity works to *reduce internal friction* while enabling an organization to *weather external friction*.

In the *Trust-Based Leadership* book I wrote:

> "The Trust-Based Leadership™ model assumes that there will be friction during all types of business operations—and many of its concepts and techniques are specifically designed to help leaders with it ... the following techniques help a leader specifically mitigate internal, *self-imposed* friction while making his or her team better equipped to deal with all types of friction:
>
> - Mission-type orders with clear commander's intent ...
>
> - Standard Operating Procedures (SOPs) and detailed planning ...
>
> - Having a clear core focus ...
>
> - Core values and a strong culture ...
>
> - Train like you fight ... "[138]

Simplicity is the key to ensuring clarity of purpose and intent. When "keeping it simple" is at the forefront as you set an objective, design a plan of action, and communicate your intent, the possibility of misunderstandings and failure are greatly diminished.

Failures of Simplicity

Unfortunately, bad examples of this Principle of War have haunted the United States' recent military interventions. Vietnam, Beirut, the second Iraq War, and the invasion of Afghanistan were all incredibly complex conflicts. And the military was hampered by internally imposed friction caused by shifting objectives and the tools used to accomplish them.

All of these interventions had limited objectives in theory that, in practice, changed and expanded once the conflicts were underway. Besides Beirut, each became a protracted conflict that involved multiple political administrations, and strategies and tactics were changed numerous times. Adaption is necessary in war—the principle of maneuver depends on it. However the level of inconsistency in these conflicts defied simplicity.

The last war in Iraq, for example, involved a ground invasion to unseat the Iraqi dictator Saddam Hussein, followed by chaos after his military was defeated. The conflict then shifted to a stabilization operation followed quickly by a counterinsurgency. Unprepared to deal with the aftermath, the U.S. military first used a hands-off strategy and tactics, then aggressive ones to fight the insurgents, and, eventually, a counterinsurgency strategy that looked far different than the preceding years.

This eventually yielded success but was followed by a rapid withdrawal once the political administration changed, and many of Iraq's stability gains were lost. Regardless of differing opinions on the conflict, it should be clear that the U.S. did not have a clear, attainable objective backed up by a straightforward strategy to achieve that objective. The U.S. political and military leadership changed and applied inconsistent strategy; tactics changed dramatically and varied considerably between units; and a frequently changing desired end state in a complex environment made it difficult to understand what victory looked like.

As a retired military professional watching from afar, I reflected on the situation our military found itself in and wondered: "What's the mission? What is the end-state required in order for American forces to declare victory?" I was unable to discern an answer. Turning to friends who still held high-level military positions, I was disheartened—though not surprised—when the answer each of them provided was essentially the same: "I know what you're asking for, Mike, and it simply doesn't exist. There is no 'American forces will achieve A, B and C in order to successfully accomplish America's military objectives in Iraq."

Contrast this with the first war with Iraq, which expelled the Iraqi Army from Kuwait and accomplished its objective after a 100-hour ground invasion. Or the 2011 mission to kill Osama bin Laden, in which 25 Navy SEALS raided a compound, accomplished the task, and were extracted successfully. Or, on a much larger scale, the U.S. war against Japan in World War II. That mission was immensely complicated, but the objective—the unconditional surrender of the Empire of Japan—was not. [139]

Simplicity failures can also beset plans, orders, and communications. The famous "Charge of the Light Brigade" serves as a shining example of bravery that inspired an epic poem. But it was also an unmitigated disaster that stemmed from a misunderstood order:

The order, written by General Airey and approved by Lord Raglan, the Commander-in-Chief in the East, reads as follows:

'Lord Raglan wishes the cavalry to advance rapidly to the front, follow the enemy & try to prevent the enemy carrying away the guns. Troop Horse Artillery may accompany. French cavalry is on your left. Immediate. R. Airey'.

Disastrously, Airey's orders were misunderstood, some of the blame resting with Captain Nolan, who took the message to the Light Brigade. The horsemen charged in the wrong direction straight towards the entire Russian army, rather than towards the guns the enemy had captured earlier. [140]

Of roughly 670 cavalrymen of the Light Brigade, "about 110 were killed and 160 were wounded, a 40 percent casualty rate." These causalities might have been avoided with a more precise definition of "advance rapidly to the front" in the order. [141]

Notably, Civil War General Ulysses S. Grant was famous for issuing unambiguous orders that would be difficult to misinterpret. And Corsican conqueror Napoleon Bonaparte was said to have made sure that all of his battle plans were simple enough for a corporal to understand. [142]

Simplicity in Business

Kelly Johnson, who as we mentioned previously is credited with coining the KISS term, outlined 14 rules for a successful project, some of them epitomize *Simplicity*:

3. The number of people having any connection with the project must be restricted in an almost vicious manner. Use a small number of good people (10% to 25% compared to the so-called normal systems).

4. A very simple drawing and drawing release system with great flexibility for making changes must be provided.

5. There must be a minimum number of reports required, but important work must be recorded thoroughly.[143]

Simplicity applies to far more than discrete projects or departments, of course. When Gary Rodkin took over as the C.E.O. of ConAgra foods in 2005, it was a "$14 billion company with more than 100 consumer and commercial brands, a food services business, and a commodity trading operation, but no common method for tracking, reporting, or analyzing results."

> Customers wanted a single face to the company, employees were frustrated with poor communication and competition among units, analysts wanted clearer numbers, and investors were unhappy with the wide duplication of functions. The fragmented organization's lack of common systems, data, and processes made it impossible to respond to those demands. So Rodkin made simplicity one of his first priorities, declaring it a hard business objective. He then invested in a series of initiatives to combat complexity, which made life easier for customers and employees—and produced millions of dollars in savings.[144]

Then there are the impacts of overly complicated orders, plans, and processes on the workforce. Brand strategy firm Siegel+Gale conducted a study that "surveyed more than 14,000 people in nine countries to understand the relationship between simple workplaces and engaged employees, and how this impacts the bottom line for companies across the globe." Among the findings:

- "Only 1 out of 5 employees find their workplace truly simple."

- 54% of employees find it easy to innovate in a simple organization vs. 2% in complex organizations.

- 95% of employees "trust their company's leadership" (vs. 69%)

- 65% are "likely to recommend someone to work at their company" (vs. 11%)

The study also found tangible benefits when it came to "bring new ideas to the table" (+31% in simple organizations), "manage their workloads" (+27%), "handle unexpected problems well" (+25%), and five other factors, including "feeling productive at work" (+21%). [145]

Essential Rules to Achieve Simplicity

Objectives. Plans. Communications. Orders and instructions. Projects. Nearly everything can benefit from being simple or, when necessarily complex, *as simple as possible*. Here are some tips to achieving this vital Principle of War:

- Evaluate the objective and the initiative required to achieve it. Identify the key factors that must be addressed.

- When developing plans, instructions, processes, and communications, pare them down to these essential elements.

- Reevaluate the plan, instructions, communications, or other items and ask whether they are as straightforward as possible while still accomplishing the objective.

- Identify clear lines of responsibility following the principle of unity of command.

- Establish and enforce a common language in communications to ensure clarity.

- Evaluate new and existing processes for unnecessary complexity. If it is found, *change them*.

Above all, keep things simple and straightforward. In business and war, this mitigates internal friction, motivates teams, improves execution, and ups the chances of success.

> *"Simplicity in planning fosters energy in execution. Strong determination in carrying through a simple idea is the surest route to success. The winning simplicity we seek, the simplicity of genius, is the result of intense mental engagement."*

—CARL VON CLAUSEWITZ

Epilogue

The modern version of the Nine Principles of War used by the U.S. military is about a century old, but the underlying philosophies and concepts are ancient. Chinese strategist SunTzu, Prussian general Carl von Clausewitz, French soldier Henri de Rohan, the Renaissance philosopher Niccolò Machiavelli, and many other martial theorists have outlined varieties of these principles. These thinkers arrived at similar conclusions because the concepts are valuable, universal, and timeless.

Militaries continue to educate soldiers about the Principles of War and employ them in modern warfare. Technology and tactics may change, but these time-tested ideas still ensure that operations have the highest chances for success.

These principles have also been applied in business—whether leaders are explicitly aware of them or not. From surprisingly successful hostile takeovers to losing market share after an inadequate defense, countless companies have succeeded because they followed the principles and failed because they didn't.

As you consider how to apply the Principles of War in your business career, keep in mind their benefits *and* limitations.

- As principles, they are not a detailed guide. When, where, and what form they take rely on translating them to actionable plans that fit your situation and need.

- As we have pointed out many times in this book, the principles do not work in isolation. Deploying resources en masse must be done in concert with considering security and economy of force, the potential for maneuver and surprise, and other concepts.

- Like their application to military planning and execution, business leaders must exercise sound judgment when applying these principles to their operations.

Wise leaders consider the Principles of War—or a version of them—when making countless decisions. But they also approach their use with an agile mind that contemplates various factors in a specific "business battlefield." Here are some questions leaders should ask themselves when evaluating each principle in a variety of situations:

Objective

- Is the objective clear, decisive, and attainable?

- If an objective is defined at the department, project, or personal level, does it support the organization's higher-level objective?

- What standards are in place to determine whether an objective needs to change?

Offensive

- Are all plans weighted toward offense?

- Does an offensive move directly support the objective? An offense for the sake of staying offensive is often pointless.

- Do I have sufficient resources to take an offensive to a successful conclusion?

Mass

- What amount of resources are required to achieve the objective?

- Do I have sufficient resources to mass toward the objective effectively?

- When resources are concentrated at this point, are there enough left over to achieve security? And is the organization agile enough to maneuver, if necessary?

Economy of Force

- Have I minimized resources devoted to secondary objectives?

- Does a secondary objective support the primary objective? If not, abandon it.

Maneuver

- What criteria are in place to determine when it is time to adapt an offensive?

- Does the organizational structure support quick adaptation? A Trust-Based Leadership™ model enables fast and effective maneuver.

- Have I created contingency plans for the "enemy's" response to a maneuver?

Unity of Command

- Is there a well-defined leadership structure—one in which each unit reports to a single leader?

- Within this framework, do leaders at all levels have the freedom to innovate to achieve their objectives while following the commander's intent? Again, this relies on Trust-Based Leadership™.

- Are all leaders competent and well-trained enough to execute within a Trust-Based Leadership™ model?

Security

- Have I identified and evaluated potential threats that would endanger mission accomplishment?

- Have I developed realistic contingency plans to address these threats?

- Have I taken steps to ensure my teammates are capable of recognizing the emerging presence of threats, and executing appropriate contingency plans?

Surprise

- Does an opportunity for surprise exist?

- Is it possible to achieve this surprise over a specific period, taking into account planning, preparation, and execution?

- If so, does surprise have the potential to achieve the objective decisively, and do I have the resources to see it through to success?

Simplicity

- Have I evaluated all orders, plans, communications, and processes to ensure that they are as complex as necessary while being as simple as possible?

- Have elements with the potential for misunderstanding been identified and addressed?

- Do all communications within an organization use a common "language?"

Many other factors should be assessed, and there are more questions leaders should ask themselves when applying these principles. Each environment is unique. But just as the Principles of War have long guided militaries to victory on the battlefield, they can point businesses toward success.

Take the time to consider each principle as you make decisions, structure an organization, and plan initiatives. This timeless knowledge can help defeat enemies—whether they are business competitors, adverse market conditions, or sudden threats to the balance sheet.

Modern business is a battlefield.
Go Forth and Lead Well!

Fidelis Leadership Group

Developing World Class Leaders

MIKE ETTORE

U.S. MARINE CORPS (RETIRED)

TRUST-BASED
LEADERSHIP™

MARINE CORPS LEADERSHIP CONCEPTS
FOR TODAY'S BUSINESS LEADERS

BONUS CONTENT

The "mission statements" of the business world are not that different from those found in military operations—defining the desired end state (intent), describing and assigning certain tasks to units and individuals, organizing and equipping the team, and ensuring timely and crisp communications. The risks associated with both "battlefields" are also similar. Although the consequences of failing to accomplish the mission during war can be far more severe in that people may die, when a company fails, whatever the reason, it can drag its employees down with it and lives could end up destroyed as well.

I am convinced that when the Principles of War are applied to business operations, successful outcomes are much more likely. That said, the application of these principles will yield minimal or no positive impact if they are not supported by sound leadership. As you know, the main role of a leader is to influence his or her team to accomplish a mission by providing purpose, direction, and inspiration. In this sense, effective leadership is the glue that binds the Principles of War together and enables them to have a holistic effect on a team and the results it achieves.

Because leadership is so critical to the effective application of the principles covered in this book, I have decided to include an entire section of another book I have published titled ***Trust-Based Leadership™: Marine Corps Leadership Concepts for Today's Business Leaders***. This section is the second of five sections that make up the book. It can help you understand some of the essential traits and skills that you and your leaders must possess and demonstrate as you strive to apply the Principles of War to good effect within your organization.

Section II:

TRUST-BASED LEADERSHIP™

Introduction:

TRUST-BASED LEADERSHIP™

Since I retired from the Marine Corps in 1998, I've effectively adapted and employed many of the concepts of Marine Corps leadership in the business world, and I've helped other business leaders do the same. My experiences have resulted in what I call the *Trust-Based Leadership™* model. It is the foundation of all of the leadership training, coaching, speaking, and writing that I do under the auspices of my company, Fidelis Leadership Group. This section of the book outlines the major *enabling philosophies* of the Trust-Based Leadership model.

I've thrown a lot of material at you so far, and now I'd like you to step back and consider it for a few minutes. View the components in sequence and at a 30,000-foot level. As you do, think of each element as a building block. Once all of the blocks are in place, the completed structure positions an organization to perform in a very specific way. In the case of the Marine Corps, this structure is used to win battles, quickly and decisively. In business, it is applied to rapidly conquer challenges and meet established goals and objectives, whatever they may be.

Let's go through these elements step by step:

- Marine recruits and officer candidates learn about and are continuously immersed in the Core Values of the Marine Corps: Honor, Courage, and Commitment. These values serve as the bedrock of everything that follows.

(1) Other values are added that form *The Marine Mindset*, which is essentially the "corporate culture" of the Corps.

(2) Being a Marine is a privilege, not a right. Marines are taught to always work as a team and seek to achieve excellence as they strive to honor the example of legendary Marines who have come before them. The Marine Corps believes that it is the best and teaches new recruits that this is true. This belief becomes a self-fulfilling prophecy.

(3) "Every Marine a Rifleman:" A fundamental identity and singular purpose are embedded in every Marine. The organization's focus—winning battles—starts with the individual and everything he or she does within a team or function is designed to support that focus.

After outlining these basic building blocks that mold every Marine, we moved on to the *science* of Marine Corps leadership:

(4) Special Trust and Confidence are placed in leaders. They have significant responsibility and accountability, and are vested with great authority in return. Marine leaders are expected to fulfill this bargain by displaying total integrity and commitment, and through seeking constant self-improvement.

(5) Leaders must care for subordinates, teach them, and learn from them. This "Teacher-Scholar 360°" concept strengthens the organization by developing leaders at *every* level—and caring for people ensures that they will in turn care for their leaders by striving for success.

(6) We discussed the Five Laws of Leadership, the 14 Leadership Traits, the 11 Leadership Principles, and The Five Pillars of Marine Corps Leadership.

(7) I explained the three fundamental responsibilities of Marine leaders in order of priority, and how they serve as a compass to guide their decisions and actions:

    o Accomplish the mission

- o Take care of your people

- o Develop the next generation of leaders

(8) I discussed the *S in BAMCIS*, explaining how supervision is the essential link between a leader's responsibility and his or her accountability—and how doing it right is necessary for delegation that allows subordinates to take initiative. Within this framework, all members of a team work to fulfill the leader's *intent* while accomplishing the mission.

Read through these items again, if you'd like. As you do, consider how they interact and build upon each other, *and what they ultimately create.*

The Marine ethos—its culture, values, and traditions—winds up transforming young, often self-centered recruits into highly motivated members of an incredibly strong team. Marine Corps leadership training forges leaders who care for their people and develop them, while displaying integrity and viewing their mandate to lead as a sacred responsibility that requires impeccable character and constant self-improvement.

Once all of these pieces are in place, it unleashes something that is incredibly powerful: A relatively nimble organization that works together to strike hard and fast.

All Marines are expected to take initiative and lead, to some degree. They have the ability to work as a team—with or in the absence of orders—to accomplish the mission, regardless of the challenges that get in their way. In other words, when the inevitable friction and fog of war appear in dangerous, chaotic environments, Marine leaders know they are expected to find a way to win—to achieve the commander's intent and effectively exploit opportunities that may surface while doing so.

This is the framework from which everything else flows. From there, the Trust-Based Leadership model and the Marine Corps experience it is based on get more specific on tactics, techniques, the methods for handling any challenges, and other elements of executing successful leadership. Let's dive in.

"In the Marine Corps, leadership by example matters most when operating in darkness and danger.

The business world is no different.

Leaders must lead by example... Always!"

—Mike Ettore

Trust-Based Leadership™

The Trust-Based Leadership™ model is a concept for winning . . . it is a business-oriented leadership doctrine based on rapid, flexible, and opportunistic decisions and actions.

The essence of Trust-Based Leadership is that all members of an organization are enabled and encouraged to take action that can generate and exploit some kind of advantage over competitors or the business environment as a means of accomplishing stated goals and objectives as effectively as possible.

Especially important are decision-making and actions in time—we generate a faster decision-making and operating tempo than our competitors or market conditions to gain a temporal advantage. It is through decisiveness and actions in all dimensions that enables a company of any size to achieve decisive superiority at the necessary time and place.

Fidelis Leadership Group
Developing World Class Leaders

fidelisleadership.com

Chapter 27

TRUST

If you had to boil down how the Marine Corps functions in one word, that might be "trust." If you were only allowed to do it in four words, they'd probably be "trust," "delegate," "execute," and "win." And while trust has always been a component of Marine Corps leadership and operations, it's taken on even more importance in the last 35 years or so.

In the mid-1980s, the Marine Corps adopted a warfighting doctrine named *Maneuver Warfare*. This doctrine depends first and foremost on a culture of absolute trust among Marines of all ranks and roles. That trust is created through the adoption and effective application of the various concepts, fundamentals, etc., that were covered in Section I. When embraced and lived by all Marines—especially those in leadership roles—every element of the Science of Marine Corps Leadership plays a role in the development of a *Culture of Trust* that is essential to the success of the Maneuver Warfare doctrine.

Maneuver Warfare is described in *MCDP (Marine Corps Doctrinal Publication) 1: Warfighting*:

> The Marine Corps concept for winning … is a warfighting doctrine based on rapid, flexible, and opportunistic maneuver. … The essence of maneuver is taking action to generate and exploit some kind of advantage over the enemy as a means of accomplishing our objectives as effectively as possible. …

> Especially important is maneuver in time—we generate a faster operating tempo than the enemy to gain a temporal advantage. It is through maneuver in all dimensions that an inferior force can achieve decisive superiority at the necessary time and place.[146]

Maneuver Warfare relies on teamwork, mission-type orders, and the delegation and supervision that enable them to be carried out. Again, all of the elements of Marine Corps culture and leadership training build this framework. If your people are unqualified and poorly motivated, and your leaders aren't very good, *it simply won't work*.

Compare this philosophy with an organization that has a very centralized, rigid, top-down structure. I'll use the Iraqi military under Saddam Hussein as an example, though we've all dealt with analogous "dictators" and the rigid-minded organizations they create in the business world.

In the Iraqi Army, non-commissioned officers and lower-level officers had very little independent authority. All of the power and the ability to make decisions were gathered toward the top of the organization. Subordinate leaders wouldn't make a move without explicit instruction, and this hesitance was reinforced by severe punishment for taking initiative. This created a slow moving, extremely reactive organization. One that, despite having 900,000 men under arms in 1990 (making it the fourth-largest army in the world), was rolled up very quickly in a fight against opposing forces who took initiative and applied Maneuver Warfare. [147]

Trust-Based Leadership™: Applying Marine Corps Leadership Concepts in Business

Since I retired from the Marine Corps in 1998, I've adapted Maneuver Warfare and other Marine leadership concepts for use in the business world. These are the main elements of the Trust-Based Leadership™ model.

There may not be an "enemy" in the business world—but there are competitors, and we all wage a daily struggle to solve problems and seize opportunities in rapidly changing, sometimes chaotic environments. Trust-based leaders and the organizations they lead are able to adapt, conquer challenges, and seize initiative at a pace that leaves other organizations—those working within a rigid, centralized model of leadership and decision-making—in the dust.

Directly adapted (and "civilianized") from the Marine Corps' definition of Maneuver Warfare, the Trust-Based Leadership model that has proven so effective for so many organizations and companies is defined as follows:

> *The Trust-Based Leadership™ model is a concept for winning ... it is a business-oriented leadership doctrine based on rapid, flexible, and opportunistic decisions and actions. ... The essence of Trust-Based Leadership is that all members of an organization are enabled and encouraged to take action that can generate and exploit some kind of advantage over competitors or the business environment as a means of accomplishing stated goals and objectives as effectively as possible.*

> *Especially important are decision-making and actions in time—we generate a faster decision-making and operating tempo than our competitors or market conditions to gain a temporal advantage. It is through decisiveness and actions in all dimensions that enables a company of any size to achieve decisive superiority at the necessary time and place.*

Reflect upon this for a moment and ask yourself, "Who wouldn't want to be part of a company that can execute and operate like this?!"

And the best part is that once the Trust-Based Leadership model is learned, implemented, and nurtured, it becomes natural and sustains itself. The companies and leaders that implement Trust-Based Leadership grow stronger and stronger over time and accrue lasting advantages and success.

When applied to any organization, the key to understanding this philosophy is the power of enterprise-level leadership by example, mutual respect and trust, speed, focus, and adaptability. A company that embraces the Trust-Based Leadership model is one that develops a culture that propels itself forward, adapts to challenges, and seizes opportunities. It continuously focuses on the development of competent leaders who can think and act independently.

Again, consider how this concept may apply to your professional environment; specifically, how a trusted subordinate could be afforded the latitude to demonstrate initiative in accomplishing a goal while still fulfilling your overall intent (and that of leaders more senior than you). Would you rather have an organization with reactive employees who can't make a move without direction? Or would you prefer a trust-based organization that has a cultural bias for action and leaders who seize and exploit appropriate opportunities?

As is often the case, Warren Buffet provides an interesting, if extreme, example. The formula of Buffet's Berkshire Hathaway is pretty simple and hugely effective: It buys successful companies and generally doesn't mess with them too much. The multinational conglomerate holding company sets goals, establishes a common culture, and gives trusted executives great latitude to accomplish their mission. It provides minimal (but effective) guidance and supervision while ensuring teammates receive adequate levels of support.

Stanford professor David Larcker and researcher Brian Tayan described Berkshire's management style in a case study for the university's Graduate School of Business:

> [U]nique was the operating structure that the company employed to manage these operations. It was a model based on extreme decentralization of operating authority, with responsibility for business performance placed entirely in the hands of local managers.
>
> While many publicly-traded corporations implemented strict controls and oversight mechanisms to ensure management performance and regulatory compliance, Berkshire Hathaway moved in the opposite direction. The company had only two main requirements for operating managers: submit financial statement information on a monthly basis and send free cash flow generated by operations to headquarters. Management was not required to meet with executives from corporate headquarters or participate in investor relations meetings; nor was it required to develop strategic plans, long-term operating targets, or financial projections.
>
> Instead, local managers were left to operate their businesses largely without supervision or corporate control. Vice Chairman Charles T. Munger described the Berkshire Hathaway system as "delegation just short of abdication."[148]

Larcker and Tayan also "surveyed approximately 80 Berkshire subsidiary CEOs to determine how Buffett's acquisition and management style translates on the ground." One respondent from a successful company under Berkshire Hathaway said "The only change is that I now discuss any major capital acquisitions with Warren. We run the business the way we always have."

Respondents reported that "their companies' performances are better under Berkshire (and even better than if they were stand-alone companies)," citing the ability to focus on long-term strategy plus the resources and brand value provided by the parent company. Respondents also mentioned the strength of a "common culture … shared across Berkshire's subsidiaries," one that is "focused on honesty, integrity, long-term orientation, and customer service."[149]

This strong, universal culture is a civilian mirror of many of the leadership and organizational principles that guide the Marine Corps, as well as the ones I and many other leaders have implemented while serving as senior executives. A culture of honesty and integrity combined with clear standards and a focused mission are essential for successfully implementing the Trust-Based Leadership™ model.

The Berkshire Hathaway example of "delegation just short of abdication" is pretty extreme, but my personal experience and study have shown that most of the very best companies in the business world all rely on *some form and degree* of decentralized command and control (C2). And trust-based organizations are only becoming more vital as businesses work in a globalized environment spanning many different locations, governments, sectors, and economies. Their success in diverse settings depends on decentralized C2 and the presence of competent, trusted leaders who take initiative and use sound judgement to achieve objectives.

Let's say your company is faced with a last-minute, time-sensitive deal that carries some personal and organizational risk. You want to have trusted leaders who will say:

> "My boss is on vacation. My regional vice president is at a conference and I cannot reach her via phone, email, or text message. My division president is on a business trip in Europe. But despite my inability to communicate with my senior leaders, I know the stated intent is to engage in deals that raise the division's gross profit. I've got a deal right in front of me. And while I usually need approval for some of the modifications

and accommodations the client is asking for in this contract, I'm going to approve it. Because I believe the boss and *his* leaders would allow me to if I were able to communicate with them. It's a good deal and it increases our gross profit."

Reflect upon this example for a moment. I can't think of a good reason why any leader would not want his subordinate leaders and other key teammates to be empowered in this way and be willing to take decisive action in the absence of guidance. This is the type of decisiveness, judgement, and bias for action found in an organization that embraces a Trust-Based Leadership model!

The subsequent chapters included in this section of the book address what I refer to as the *Enabling Concepts of Trust-Based Leadership.* As you read each chapter, I encourage you to remember that <u>the fundamental element in each of them is trust</u>; the complete and unshakable trust that is promoted, developed, and maintained among all members of a trust-based organization.

"Leadership is an art in which the artist can continue to improve throughout his or her entire life."

—Mike Ettore

Chapter 28

MISSION TACTICS

Maneuver Warfare relies on an operating philosophy known as *"Mission Tactics"* and an associated technique of issuing guidance to subordinates that is referred to as *"Mission Orders."* Mission orders are used by Marine leaders to assign missions, goals, objectives, and tasks to individuals.

This technique depends on and enables trust. And it's essential to the effective delegation of all types of missions to members of a Marine unit. It also promotes the concept of accomplishing the mission at all costs, even if junior leaders have to deviate from established plans and orders to adapt to rapidly changing circumstances on the battlefield.

Bear with me as you read about the Maneuver Warfare-related concepts, techniques, and examples in this and other chapters in this book. They may seem esoteric or only applicable to the military—but please keep in mind that I've successfully adapted and employed all of them in the business world. And I've taught many other business leaders to do the same.

Mission Tactics

MCDP (Marine Corps Doctrinal Publication) 1: Warfighting defines mission tactics as follows:

> Mission tactics serve as a contract between senior and subordinate. The senior agrees to provide subordinates with the

support necessary to help them accomplish their missions but without necessarily prescribing their actions. The senior is obligated to provide the guidance that allows subordinates to exercise proper judgement and initiative.

The subordinate is obligated to act in conformity with the intent of the senior. The subordinate agrees to act responsibly and loyally and not to exceed the proper limits of authority. Mission tactics require subordinates to act with "top sight"—a grasp of how their actions fit into the larger situation. In other words, subordinates must always think above their own levels in order to contribute to the accomplishment of the higher mission.[150]

Marine Corps Major Peter E. Higgins also summarized mission tactics well in a 1990 thesis for the Command and Staff College (CSC): "Historical Applications of Maneuver Warfare in the 20th Century." As you read the following, consider how this concept can be applied in the business world (emphasis added):

> **Mission tactics are also called "trust tactics".** Leaders are expected to make decisions without constant supervision and without asking for permission as long as their decisions are within the framework of **the commander's intent**. Mission tactics replace control with guidance and allow the subordinate leader to do without question or doubt whatever the situation requires—**even the disobedience of orders was not inconsistent with this philosophy**. ...
>
> The situation may dictate changing the mission to comply with the commander's intent. Of course, we want initiative on the battlefield, and when subordinates know the commander's intent, it will synchronize their efforts to support the will of their commander. **In the absence of orders, a subordinate will still know what to do if he knows his commander's intent.** He now has the latitude to take advantage of fleeting opportunities.[151]

Commander's Intent

The key term in the example cited is *"Commander's Intent."* The Marine Corps defines it as follows (emphasis added):

> We achieve this harmonious initiative in large part through the use of the commander's intent, **a device designed to help subordinates understand the larger context of their actions**. The purpose of providing intent is to allow subordinates to exercise judgement and initiative—to depart from the original plan when the unforeseen occurs—in a way that is consistent with higher commanders' aims.
>
> There are two parts to any mission: the task to be accomplished and the reason or intent behind it. The intent is thus a part of every mission. The task describes the action to be taken while the intent describes the purpose of the action.
>
> The task denotes what is to be done, and sometimes when and where; the intent explains why. <u>Of the two, the intent is predominant.</u>
>
> While a situation may change, making the task obsolete, the intent is more lasting and continues to guide our actions. Understanding the intent of our commander allows us to exercise initiative in harmony with the commander's desire.[152]

There are three major benefits to setting clear commander's intent.

First, it fundamentally gets everyone on the same page, aligning the organization toward a goal.

Second, knowing the "larger context of their actions" gives subordinates the ability to adapt effectively while carrying out orders.

Finally, by communicating commander's intent, Marine leaders ensure that their subordinates are better informed of what the "big picture" looks like, and this results in them becoming more engaged and vested in the successful accomplishment of the mission. It also serves to inspire them, as they fully understand the key role they and their teammates are playing in any operation.

Examples of Commander's Intent in Combat

In this first example, a Marine infantry captain is ordered to capture a bridge and to subsequently occupy specific defensive positions on its eastern side. He's told that the commander's intent is to prevent the enemy from moving forces across the river at that specific location, while preserving the bridge so Marine and allied units can use it to cross the river during future operations.

Once he and his unit seize the bridge, the captain discovers that the terrain isn't as expected. The specific defensive position he was directed to occupy on the eastern side of the river is not conducive to preventing the enemy from crossing the bridge. He determines that his unit will need to move to the western side of the river and occupy better defensive positions to protect the bridge while simultaneously preventing enemy forces from crossing it.

In this example, the captain had been issued orders that became unrealistic once he was able to actually see the terrain on the eastern side of the bridge. And he appropriately adapted his tactics within the framework of the order to accomplish the commander's intent; both the immediate intent (prevent enemy crossing) and the longer-term intent (maintain a way for Marine and allied units to subsequently use the bridge).

Here's another example of commander's intent being used in a combat situation: When Marine infantry units are engaged in combat operations, junior Marines have historically been ordered to dig *a lot* of fighting holes and other defensive positions, which is difficult, back-breaking work done with small shovels. Often, after these Marines have been working for a good amount of time and have expended a lot of energy digging, they receive word that the unit is moving to a new location where they will have to begin working on *new* fighting holes. As you might imagine, the morale of these Marines often suffers; they begin to feel like pawns on a chessboard that they cannot see.

At the same time these Marines are preparing their new defensive positions, some of them are also routinely ordered to man forward-observation posts for hours, often at the expense of precious sleep and recovery time. Simply put, they're placed under stress and they're in the dark. Marines may have already been fighting enemy forces for days or weeks without adequate sleep, rest, food, or water, and they don't know exactly what their unit is trying to accomplish—nor what their particular role is in the tactical plan.

Consider the difference in these Marines' energy, motivation, and engagement if their sergeant had communicated the fact that an enemy force has been spotted moving in the unit's direction, and *the commander's intent is to guard the unit's left flank*.

These Marines are going to dig much deeper fighting holes and remain a lot more attentive while on watch at the observation posts, simply because they know the enemy situation and the commander's intent. It conveys the context of the difficult tasks they are being ordered to execute, and the gravity of failing to execute them well.

An Example of Commander's Intent in Business

In this example, two sales managers are told they must complete tedious and time-consuming end-of-week sales reports. One is told "Just do it, the Chief Sales Officer wants to review these reports no later than 2 p.m. every Friday."

The other sales manager is told the intent of the guidance from the corporate office: "We recently had several discrepancies between what some of our clients understood and expected as deliverables and what we thought we were contracted for and paid to deliver. In the end, we wound up modifying these contracts to specify a lower level of service, and some of your sales reps' monthly commissions will be affected. We need a way to identify and reconcile any problems quickly so we can ensure your teammates are paid correctly."

The second sales manager understands the intent and the importance of the end-of-week reporting. He's probably going to work with more enthusiasm and better tolerate doing that boring task, whereas the less-informed sales manager may not. In addition, there is a chance that well-informed teammates at any level—not just the leaders—may suggest *a better way* to *fulfill* the intent to solve this reporting issue.

An individual sales rep may say to her boss, "Hey, I think we can create and fill out an automated form with the exact terms of the contract upon the close of any sale; integrate this form into our client management system and accounting platforms to reconcile invoices with contracts. Or instead of doing this custom, weekly report, why don't we add these simple fields to current reporting that's already filled out as sales are made?"

Simply knowing the intent often spurs innovation or effective suggestions from within a team, because its members understand *why* they are being asked to do something.

Commander's Intent and Mission-Type Orders are Adaptable to any Organization

The higher up you go in any trust-based organization, the more important delegation becomes, and the more that delegation relies on clearly communicated commander's intent and mission-type orders.

A janitor is not going to require a mission-type order to clean the hallways, meetings rooms, and bathrooms on the third floor of an office building every night. In contrast, a salesperson selling technical solutions and support services will need this type of adaptive guidance to do his job effectively.

In that example, the intent of a sales team order could be "we are going to increase top-line growth (gross revenue) for the next two quarters."

Whatever the aim—increase gross revenue or net profit, roll out a new IT system by the end of Q3, or design and implement an effective marketing campaign—a leader must define the mission and the standards, *and* set the intent. Within that framework, subordinates can strive to meet their goals while *always* keeping their decisions in line with the intent.

That salesperson in an effectively led trust-based organization will be someone capable of thinking: "My boss is on vacation, but I know the intent is to increase our gross revenue. I've got a deal here that requires some adaptations of how we do things; but those changes are minor, and this increases our gross revenue. Let's do it."

Now, this example may seem a bit simplistic, but I assure you: There are countless companies in which the salesperson does not have the latitude to make that deal if he is unable to receive approval from the boss. Lacking the freedom to make decisions that support the intent of his leaders, this salesperson will likely watch in dismay as the contract remains unsigned and is lost to a nimble and empowered competitor.

Take an honest look at your own situation, be it as an individual contributor, a team leader or a senior executive. Are people in your organization trained and enabled to make decisions that will benefit the company? Or are they operating in a *"do only what you are told to do"* environment?

If you don't like your answers, take action and make things right!

Micromanagement is Fatal to Mission Tactics

A **non**-mission-type order doesn't just communicate the mission and the intent; it prescribes exactly what an individual must do. The only settings where this may be appropriate are those at the lowest levels of organizations; when an individual is needed for a task (for the moment) but does not have the knowledge, experience, or skills to take initiative; or for vital tasks which require consistent and specific processes and procedures.

Now, in some instances, various operations and tasks simply *must* be executed in a rather rigid or prescribed manner, often with a high level of supervision from senior leaders. There's nothing wrong with this, as long as the situation truly warrants such detailed guidance, direction, and continuous scrutiny from leaders. An extreme example of the latter would be the decision to initiate the launch sequence for a nuclear missile. You sure as hell don't want to see much front-line initiative in this situation!

In the aforementioned sales example, however, a mission-type order to a salesperson might look like this:

"Our goal is to increase top-line growth (gross revenue) for the next two quarters. We would like to do this by focusing on businesses in these four industries: hospitals, surgical centers, physical therapy practices, and orthopedic surgical partnerships."

A **non**-mission-type order would be something along the lines of this:

"We want to increase top-line growth. Here is a list of 13 companies; call on them within the next 5 days and in this order. Only accept deals that generate at least 26% gross margin. There can be no deviation from our established billing rates and customer support procedures."

The leader issuing this order, who may not even be based in the same zip code, is dictating to a salesperson—who best understands her geographic market and the companies in it—exactly how she must go about accomplishing the mission. That salesperson may be thinking, "Of the 13 companies on your list, four of them just had massive layoffs and are focused on cost reductions. We're probably not going to be able to sell them anything for quite some time!"

As a Trust-Based Leader, <u>don't try to dictate every aspect of how your teammates will accomplish the mission.</u> Formulate mission-type orders *with prior input* from those who are going to be receiving them, as well as *subsequent input* that may require you to modify the order moving forward. Let the front-line leaders and teammates you trust interpret your intent and use their initiative to make things happen.

Of course, there's that word again: *trust.* Mission tactics, mission orders, and commander's intent are *very* powerful techniques, but they are useless (or worse) if the individuals who are executing them cannot be trusted to exercise sound judgement and appropriate initiative.

As with many things in this book, the sum is greater than its individual parts. Each element of the Trust-Based Leadership™ model works in concert with others to make great things possible. Specifically, the use of mission tactics and mission-type orders requires a culture of integrity and excellence, an active effort to develop and delegate to subordinate leaders, and leaders who use judgement to put the right people in the right positions.

"Great leaders apply the science
of leadership in an artful manner,
consistently achieve superior
results, and develop other leaders
who can do the same."

—Mike Ettore

Chapter 29

DECENTRALIZED COMMAND & CONTROL

Maneuver Warfare and the derivative Trust-Based Leadership™ model rely on a philosophy of decentralized command and control (C2). In addition to the benefit of empowering leaders to devise adaptable solutions, decentralized C2 creates much *faster* ones. The Marine Corps cites this quick pace as the most important element of Maneuver Warfare in the "Philosophy of Command" section of *Warfighting*:

> It is essential that our philosophy of command support the way we fight. First and foremost, in order to generate the tempo of operations we desire and to best cope with the uncertainty, disorder, and fluidity of combat, command and control must be decentralized.

> That is, subordinate commanders must make decisions on their own initiative, based on their understanding of their senior's intent, rather than passing information up the chain of command and waiting for the decision to be passed down.

> Further, a competent subordinate commander who is at the point of decision will naturally better appreciate the true situation than a senior commander some distance removed. Individual initiative and responsibility are of paramount importance. The principal means by which we implement

> decentralized command and control is through the use of mission tactics ...[153]

In both the Marine Corps and the business world, decentralized C2 and mission tactics—that implicit contract between leaders and subordinates to fulfill the commander's intent—promote an adaptive *culture of execution* in which individuals at all levels seize on opportunities and find a way to get the job done quickly and effectively.

The Marine Corps instills this culture because when tactical radios and other communication networks get jammed or are otherwise rendered inoperable, the senior commanders or key leaders are killed or incapacitated, or whatever other challenges and obstacles arise, the remaining leaders—the junior officers, SNCOs, and NCOs—can quickly assume more senior leadership roles and continue the mission.

On the battlefield, it is also necessary to seize and keep momentum. The Marine Corps trains its leaders to know when to press the initiative against an enemy in the absence of orders, as long as doing so fulfills the commander's intent. The previously mentioned scenario of a Marine captain exercising sound judgement and initiative while seizing and defending a bridge is an example of this.

The business battlefield has similar needs, though the stakes are obviously not as high as those in an actual combat zone. Leaders get sick or have family issues that cause them to be absent; they take vacations and some of them suddenly resign or are asked to exit the company.

If this happens in a *centralized* C2 organization, what happens when that "hands-on" leader is suddenly gone or unavailable? Subordinates are unused to having the latitude and authority to exercise their judgement and initiative, and business operations may become inefficient or even paralyzed. While the operational tempo and decision-making cycle in most companies tend to happen at a much slower pace than they do in a combat scenario, *decentralized* C2 enables members of a company that embraces the Trust-Based Leadership model to strike while the iron is hot and exploit fleeting opportunities.

The Marine Corps explicitly states the key to making decentralized C2 work:

> **Our philosophy requires competent leadership at all levels.**
> A centralized system theoretically needs only one competent
> person, the senior commander, who is the sole authority. A
> decentralized system requires leaders at all levels to demon-
> strate sound and timely judgement. Initiative becomes an
> essential condition of competence among commanders.[154]

Decentralized C2 and the need for competent leaders with a bias for action are becoming even more important in the modern business environment, which continues to become more global, culturally diverse, and technologically and operationally complex.

The decentralized C2 approach championed by the Trust-Based Leadership model provides leaders throughout the chain of command the ability to use their judgement. They can deviate from established plans, policies, and procedures to adapt to local political, economic, and market conditions, culture, weather, or any other unique aspects of the environment that affect business operations.

Things may be quite different in the western region of a company versus the eastern region, for example. And differences and associated complexities become exponentially greater when companies with global operations have to navigate different national governments, laws, languages, and cultures.

In a well-designed decentralized C2 organization, a company's overall mission, goals, and objectives (commander's intent) are typically the same throughout the organization, but the regional vice presidents, local managers, and other leaders have the authority to decide to do some things differently—as long as they're all striving to achieve the stated intent.

Fortunately, technology—including the broad range of communication systems and other business platforms—has greatly enabled the concept of decentralized C2 and the effective supervision needed to make it work. In today's business world, worldwide communication is instantaneous, and many teams can almost seamlessly work together at great distances from each other. This supports an unprecedented degree of decentralized C2 and its associated flexibility, responsiveness, initiative, and decisiveness at all levels.

Examples of Successful Decentralized C2

First, it's important to recognize that very few successful organizations are *completely* decentralized. Highly-directive and appropriately rigid orders and guidance still flow through the chain of command in the Marine Corps when necessary. And even companies under Warren Buffet's highly decentralized Berkshire Hathaway model of "delegation just short of abdication" are beholden to a common culture and must still submit financial and operational reports and perform other tasks that leave little, if any, room for deviation or modification.

The traditional franchise business model provides an example of a mix of decentralized and centralized C2. National or international brands such as Matco Tools, Pearle Vision, McDonald's, or Chick-fil-A set specific, very detailed standards. In the case of a restaurant franchise, for example, the corporate leadership determines the menu, recipes, portion sizes, and more. But individual franchisees often have the flexibility to modify some of their business practices to account for local conditions, as long as they remain within the broad intent and the standards set by corporate headquarters.

The Johnson & Johnson Company is a famous example of highly decentralized command and control. J&J has over "200 operating companies that produce consumer goods such as baby shampoo and medical products." This diverse structure is unified by the company's "Credo," which "states that the company's primary responsibility is to the people who use their products, secondary responsibility is to their employees, tertiary responsibility is to the communities they operate in, and final responsibility is to their shareholders. And as a result, J&J historically has deployed an operating strategy to invest in people and innovation, both through their own employees and external parties through acquisitions."[155]

In 2008, then Chairman and CEO William Weldon had this to say about Johnson & Johnson's structure in an interview with the Wharton School of Business:

> I think J&J is probably the reference company for being decentralized. There are challenges to it, and that is you may not have as much control as you may have in a centralized company. But the good part of it is that you have wonderful leaders, you have great people that you have a lot of confidence and faith in and they run the businesses.

If you look at Japan, for example, we have the local management running the companies. They understand the consumer,
they understand the people they are dealing with, and they
understand the government and the needs in the marketplace. Whereas it's very hard to run it from the US and to think
that we would know enough to be able to do this. And so, I
think it really affords us a lot of opportunities by being decentralized; what you do lose is control. But, with our credo and
the value system that we work under, we feel very confident
about our leadership and our management—and you have to
have trust and confidence in them.[156]

Reflect upon Mr. Weldon's comments and contemplate how beneficial it
would be if your company, department, or team could operate in a trust-
based environment with a decentralized C2 similar to Johnson & Johnson.

Another great example: Back in 1999, Illinois Tool Works was dubbed "The
most decentralized company in the world" by *Forbes*. At that time, ITW had
"$6 billion in sales, [but was] broken into 400 units with an average revenue
of just $15 million." Fast forward to 2016, and the company had grown to
over 50,000 employees and $16.6 billion in sales. Here's how its decentral-
ization worked:

There aren't any companywide, preset benchmark profit
goals, such as those GE and AlliedSignal impose. Instead
top management imposes standards based on a particular unit's competition. Each general manager must usually
submit to grillings about six times a year by one of Farrell's
seven executive vice presidents: "Why don't you have that
account? Why does our competitor have it? What will you
do to get it?"

When a unit starts to outperform—or underperform—the
competition, Farrell splits it into more pieces, usually along
tightly focused product lines. This corporate mitosis, Farrell
argues, acts to capitalize better on what's working—or to iso-
late what's wrong. "When you separate the pieces, you can
grow faster than if you keep them together, and that growth
far outstrips the duplicate costs," he says.[157]

Various models of decentralization C2 can be applied to the entire structure of a company or the way individual departments are organized and interact within a company, all the way down to how small teams of employees work on specific projects. To be successful, the exact nature and level of decentralization often varies according to the unit's size and goals. Here is a good rule of thumb: Companies can effectively utilize the concept of decentralized C2 to the extent they can create and maintain a strong culture of execution, set high standards, and develop effective leaders—who in turn develop other effective leaders capable of sustaining the culture while achieving stated goals and objectives.

The benefits of decentralized C2 are varied but a huge one is *organizational resilience*. Nicolas Bloom, a Professor of Economics at Stanford University, conducted research that proves the worth of decentralized command and control:

> "Decentralization helps firms perform better, particularly in bad times," says Bloom, coauthor of "Never Waste a Good Crisis? Growth and Decentralization in the Great Recession," a working paper.
>
> Bloom's paper, coauthored with Philippe Aghion of Harvard University, Raffaella Sadun of Harvard Business School, and John Van Reenen of the Centre for Economic Performance at London School of Economics, examined company performance just before and during the Great Recession and found that firms that decentralized their decision making had lower falls in their sales and faster increases in their productivity than those with a centralized structure.
>
> Uncertainty rises and conditions change quickly during a recession, increasing the need for companies to respond to such dynamic times, the researchers say. That's more likely to occur when managers are empowered to make decisions instead of waiting for orders to filter down from the executive suite. "It's really costly to have big response times, so that would suggest pushing decisions down," Bloom says.
>
> These findings, Bloom says, sharply contrast with the long-standing notion that centralized firms perform more strongly during recessions because they allow C-suite executives to

make the tough and unpleasant decisions about plant closures, layoffs, and other types of aggressive cost-cutting, assumed to be the primary survival strategy in a downturn. Although the researchers examined midsized manufacturing companies, the findings apply to various industries, says Bloom.[158]

An Example of *Centralized* Command and Control Failure

A few years ago, one of my executive coaching clients told me about a situation in which he left a high-level executive position to take a job at another company—and the new leader who was appointed to replace him did massive damage to the department, effectively setting it back several years in productivity and efficiency.

When my client left this company, senior executives, who had years before embraced the concept of decentralized C2, decided not to replace him. Instead, they chose to break up the very large organization he had led and assign various departments and functions to other executives. My client supported this plan, with one exception: one of the leaders they had chosen to inherit some of his departments had a very "hands-on" and dictatorial style. My client warned senior leaders that this person's oppressive and micromanaging leadership style would likely clash with some of the leaders and teams he was about to assume control of.[159]

This new executive took the reins of several previously successful departments and teams and immediately began making unnecessary and sweeping changes. He demanded that a large number of highly capable remote employees who'd been working offsite for many years convert to working in-office at all times; he centralized all decision-making, declaring that no one could authorize a project, make a decision, or take the slightest form of initiative without consulting him first; and he integrated his newly inherited teams into his *existing* group. This was a problem because his longtime employees were used to his oppressive style, had been part of an average-performing department (at best), and suffered from poor morale.

As you might imagine, these changes caused a precipitous drop in morale among the teams this executive took over, resulting in rapid and massive turnover of high-quality employees who had been excellent performers for years. Many of them resigned within several weeks of exposure to the dictatorial leadership style of their new executive.

Sadly, this executive was in an automobile accident a few months later and he sustained very serious injuries that put him in the hospital for several months. Because he had deliberately trained his subordinate leaders to only act on his orders and directions (with dire ramifications for those who dared do otherwise), they simply *didn't know what to do* now that he was absent.

The recent loss of so many quality, long-tenured employees, the vast intellectual capital that left with them, and the department's culture of all decisions being made by this executive effectively paralyzed everything once he was gone. Operations ground to a halt and the entire company began to suffer from the fact that various support units were no longer capable of providing adequate support.

Eventually, another executive was assigned to take temporary control of the organization while the injured executive was recovering. He quickly discovered that the department was used to a domineering and dictatorial manner—that leaders and key players had been trained to never make a decision unless they obtained permission and detailed guidance.

Sorting out this mess took far more time and effort than the senior executives had ever imagined it would, and the company lost significant revenue and suffered serious operational decline for months. Worse, more quality, longtime employees quit in disgust, taking with them vast operational expertise that was impossible to replicate in the near-term.

Eventually, the injured executive returned to work and he immediately attempted to reinstate his oppressive style of leadership. This didn't go over well with his teammates, as they had become accustomed to more freedom and latitude under their temporary leader. Numerous complaints flooded the human resources department. Many of these were about his oppressive leadership style, whereas some cited verbal abuse and other instances of poor leadership. Within several weeks of his return, senior executives finally took action and fired the executive.

The worst part of this story is that by the time this individual was "found out" to be an ineffective leader, he had caused several dozen extremely valuable teammates to leave the company. Many of his ill-conceived reorganization efforts had also created great turmoil within teams that had performed very well for many years. In other words, this executive's ego, controlling personality, and micromanaging leadership resulted in him "fixing what wasn't broken." In several instances and almost immediately, the poorly reorganized teams showed a steep decline in effectiveness.

I have witnessed many situations like this in both the business world and the Marine Corps. A leader who hoards authority and decision-making almost always sets the organization up for failure. Subordinate leaders and key players are not empowered, nor do they learn to take initiative. And if the centralized, "hands-on" leader is out of commission, the entire unit typically devolves into paralysis and chaos.

A Marine battalion commander has no business micromanaging daily rifle counts in the company armories (I've seen some do this), and a senior executive should not be reviewing and approving every individual employee's vacation schedule and daily work tasks (I've also seen this, which is a gross misuse of an executive's time).

Within your own sphere of leadership—whether that is as a senior executive or the leader of a three-person team—invest in your people's development and strive to decentralize command and control, to the extent that it makes sense. Do not strictly centralize authority and decision-making in yourself, and resist the centralization of it in others. Doing the latter may produce short-term results from some individuals who cling to this authority; but it often ends poorly when someone is taken out of commission, or a big decision must be made quickly.

"The true test of your leadership begins when you're gone."

—Mike Ettore

Chapter 30

PRIORITY OF EFFORT

In Maneuver Warfare, great emphasis is placed on leaders stating clear and concise mission statements, and they use various planning and communication techniques to ensure their units are focused on what's important.

Marine leaders often have to deal with conflicting priorities. Whether they are operating in high-stress training exercises or combat operations, there's often an overload of competing demands with not enough time to address all of them. Thus, leaders are taught to remain focused on the assigned mission and commander's intent, and to assess and prioritize the tasks that are most relevant to mission accomplishment.

When faced with rapidly changing situations and established plans that are no longer relevant, Marine leaders must remain calm and consciously avoid becoming overwhelmed. They know the onus is on them to assess the situation, adjust priorities, and issue new orders and guidance to their teammates.

As always, great attention is paid to the proper application of the "S" in "BAMCIS" by leaders throughout the chain of command. This supervision ensures that the prioritized goals and objectives critical to mission accomplishment are being adequately executed.

A particularly effective way to prioritize and execute under pressure is to stay at least a step or two ahead of real-time problems. To "pull themselves off the firing line," leaders at the top of the organization step back and focus on maintaining the strategic picture. This perspective helps correctly set priorities for the team.

Just as in combat, priorities in business can rapidly shift or become irrelevant. When this happens, leaders must communicate that shift to the rest of the team—both up and down the chain of command.

Application to Business

The Trust-Based Leadership™ model utilizes these same general concepts. Trust-Based Leaders must be capable of assessing the mission, the commander's intent, and individual goals and objectives to create a prioritized sequence of actions that must be executed to achieve success.

There are many superb methods and techniques that leaders can use to do this, and I encourage readers to explore this topic in depth by reading books, articles, and other resources that are specifically dedicated to helping you gain clarity and prioritize. For the purposes of this chapter, we are discussing the high-level concept of Priority of Effort. Thus, only the major elements are covered.

Trust-Based Leaders will generally take the following two-phased approach as they assess a mission and the commander's intent; prioritize goals, objectives, and tasks; and create a plan of attack that allows for flexibility and initiative during its execution.

Phase I: Assessment, Prioritization and Planning

1. Review the Mission and the Commander's Intent: The leader must ensure that he and his subordinates have a thorough understanding of the mission, its objectives, and the commander's intent. Leaders are responsible for asking questions of their leaders until these elements are clear.

2. Create a List of Goals, Objectives, and Associated Tasks: This is a draft of these items; one that will be refined as the mission progresses and new challenges and priorities are identified.

3. Assess and Identify What's Critical vs. Important: Critical tasks are non-negotiable unless something substantially changes. Important tasks follow in prioritization but also must be completed.

4. Create a Prioritized Task List: Order tasks by their status (critical, important, or desired) as well as when they can be completed (some critical tasks may require other steps before they can be accomplished).

5. Create and Issue the Plan: Design it clearly and only make it as complex as it needs to be. Ensure that all of the plan's executors understand their role, the mission, and the commander's intent.

Phase II: Execution

6. Execute All Tasks: Get it done by issuing mission-type orders.

7. Be Vigilant, Flexible, Adaptable, and Decisive: Vigilance includes leaders properly supervising teammates (The S in BAMCIS) to ensure executors diligently fulfill their role. Flexibility, adaptability, and decisiveness are relevant because leaders must be capable of overcoming unforeseen obstacles and alter course when necessary.

8. Deviate from Plans When Necessary: No plan survives its execution 100 percent intact. New challenges and scenarios will arise that call for a change. When this happens, a leader must be able to recognize that an adaptation is needed and decisively issue orders.

9. Remain Focused on the Mission and Commander's Intent: Of course, it all comes down to the mission and the intent of your senior leaders. Never let go of this focus at any stage of the process.

10. Determine Follow-on Actions, If Necessary: What could have been done better? What still needs to be done? And what can be done to take advantage of new opportunities that are either beyond the scope of the original mission and commander's intent, or augment them. Powerful organizations are relentless about relevant follow-on actions.

In addition to the leadership philosophies and principles covered in previous chapters, all of the *enabling concepts* contained in the remaining chapters of this section directly and indirectly affect a leader's ability to prioritize and execute plans.

Chapter 31

SIMPLICITY

Combat is complicated and confusing, to put it mildly. But so is business and, for that matter, life. Running any organization or tackling a new initiative involves numerous moving parts, processes, and people. This truism—that everything is complex—drives the need to effectively manage the human element by keeping things simple.

Marine Corps leaders are trained that when it comes to leading their Marines in all types of environments, the concept that "simple is better" is one that they ignore at their peril. They are ingrained with the philosophy that they must, to the extent possible, ensure that plans, operations, tactics, techniques, orders, and communications should be kept as straightforward as possible.

This simplicity enables quick understanding and execution, both of which enhance the likelihood of success during rapidly changing and chaotic environments.

Simplicity in Everything, Including Plans, Orders, Communications ... and *Purpose*

The need for simplicity applies to nearly every element of leadership, but let's first think of its value in formulating plans. The plan (and the orders that flow from it) must be uncomplicated enough to be easily understood and executed by numerous people. It also has to be sufficiently straightforward to weather the inevitable changes that challenge its viability, such as casualties among key leaders, failing radios, or the intangible confusion that is the "Fog of War."

The plan, say, for a Marine unit to "secure that bridge" must be simple and clear enough so that the people carrying it out easily understand the objective and the commander's intent, while not being hamstrung by self-imposed complications when things don't go as expected. To put it another way, simplicity reduces *internal* friction which enables Marines to better handle *external* friction—a concept we'll detail more in a subsequent chapter.

Napoleon Bonaparte is considered one of the greatest military leaders in history, and his success largely stemmed from certain exceptional leadership qualities. Notably, he had the ability to intensely motivate his soldiers and adapt much quicker than his enemies using a 19th-Century version of maneuver warfare. But a famous story known as "Napoleon's corporal" implies that he valued simplicity as well:

> The story goes that during the battle planning stages Napoleon would have one of his … corporals shine his boots, with the understanding that he knew the corporal would be listening in on his conversation with the rest of his commanders. Following the brief he gave to the other leaders in his army, Napoleon would look to the corporal and ask him if the plans made sense. If he answered "yes" then they would go forward with the plans. But if he did not understand them then Napoleon and his staff would make changes or draft new plans.[160]

This story may or may not be apocryphal but it's wise, regardless. Good leadership requires plans and orders to be clear and specific, hence the military's emphasis on the principle and its use of various tools to accomplish it. One of these tools that's taught to leaders is the five-paragraph operations order, often known by the acronym **SMEAC**. Marine Corps Officer Candidates School (OCS) describes it as follows (emphasis added):

> **S**ituation. The Situation paragraph provides details on both friendly and enemy personnel operating in your area of operations. We combine our understanding of the terrain with an understanding of the enemy force we are facing, and what friendly support we may have around us to help our decision-making process for finding our solution.

M̲ission. A short statement containing all five "W's". **When** is **who**, doing **what**, to **whom**, and most important of all, the **why**. This is the problem that we have to determine the solution for. Using all of the information we have at this point, we determine a course of action to accomplish the mission.

E̲xecution. This is where we communicate the plan (solution) for our problem (the mission) we are tasked to accomplish. Starting from our present location, we brief how we get to the point where the "what" has been accomplished that leads to the "why" of the operation. We provide enough detail to direct how to accomplish the mission without being too detailed where we lose initiative from subordinates. We imply discretion to subordinates in determining how they accomplish their tasks.

A̲dministration & Logistics. Providing some of the smaller details of the operation, this paragraph focuses on medical issues, Enemy Prisoner of War handling, food, water, and ammunition needed to accomplish the mission. We remember the details involved in this portion through the use of four "B's": **Beans, Bullets, Band-aids, and Bad Guys.**

C̲ommand & Signal. Here we wrap up the order by discussing how we will communicate key events throughout the operation. We also discuss where key personnel are going to be located, and what the order will be for succession of command in the event the unit leader becomes a casualty.

Marine leaders are taught this and other planning templates because "Standard order formats expedite understanding, communication, prevent omissions and facilitate ready reference." Further, "A short, simple order that conveys your will is superior to a lengthy, complicated order."[161]

As another example, communications also require clarity and simplicity. The Marine Corps (and the US military as a whole) uses standardized brevity codes in communications that leverage a common language. Take these examples of multiservice brevity code words used in air-to-air, air-to-surface, surface-to-air, and surface-to-surface engagements:

- Abort: Cease and desist an action or mission.

- Champagne: Specifies an attack of three distinct groups with two in front and one behind.

- Cleared Hot: Ordnance release is authorized.

- Go secure: Use encrypted voice communications.

- Gorilla: A large enemy force of indeterminate numbers and formation has been spotted.

- LZ: Landing Zone

- Brevity: This is a directive call indicating the radio frequency is becoming saturated, degraded or jammed and briefer transmissions must follow.[162]

Brevity codes can communicate *a lot* of information in an extremely simple, efficient manner. When used effectively, they greatly reduce the length of messages and minimize the possibility of confusion among units operating on the same battlefield.

Simplicity is not limited to these two examples. It's an essential part of almost all aspects of Marine Corps leadership as well as the Trust-Based Leadership™ model that derives from it.

This directness is enabled by having a common operating language, simple plans and orders, straightforward processes, and clear standard operating procedures (SOPs)—all of which will be covered in more detail in the following chapters. These elements, of course, have similar value in the civilian world. And never forget that the quest for simplicity applies to *nearly everything*—including your basic purpose and mission.

Application to Business

When I first joined Kforce, I knew nothing about the staffing industry. As I began studying the nuances of the business, I started getting lost in vast detail. The various policies, practices, systems, and tools that our recruiters and account managers used to conduct business on a daily basis seemed hopelessly complicated.

Sensing my confusion, Larry Stanczak, my boss at the time, sat me down and said something similar to what one of my previous Marine Corps leaders would have said: "Mike, don't get consumed in the minutia. At its core, our business is very simple: we interact with companies that need individuals with certain skills to help them with their business. We find these individuals and connect them with the companies. If a company feels that the individual is a good fit, the company agrees to hire them. No matter what else we do, everything is supposed to support this simple process of finding the right candidates for companies that are in need of their skill sets."

I never forgot this lesson throughout the rest of my career with Kforce. I always viewed operations, projects, systems, or whatever element from the perspective of how they would enable and simplify our people's ability to find qualified candidates and place them with companies that needed them.

When I transitioned from the Marine Corps into a role as a business leader in 1999, I took the concept of simplicity with me—especially the techniques associated with planning and communications. I applied them to practically everything I was involved with from a leadership and operational perspective. Though I was new to business, I had a gut-feeling that these techniques could be used effectively in this new setting. And I quickly realized that this instinct was correct.

In my executive role, I found that despite not having the *combat* rationale for clarity, brevity, and precision, these guidelines had just as much benefit in the modern business world. And they still applied to all types of communications and plans.

My teammates at every level responded well to the methods I'd learned and used in the Marine Corps. Even better, others at Kforce adopted these techniques. Within a couple of years, the entire company was using many of them, and they enhanced our internal and external planning and communication competence. Most of my civilian counterparts had received no formal training on planning and organizing tasks, projects, or business operations. Thus, when I taught them some of these tools, they saw that they worked and seized upon them.

There are many management concepts and techniques that can help a business leader keep things simple and, again, the chapters following this one will get into some of them. For now, I just want you to understand the concept of simplicity and its value in almost everything you do. Simplicity should be the goal in all types of operations and tasks, from planning and executing a big new IT project to the organizational design of a department to the individual emails you send every day.

- Keeping things simple ensures common understanding and consistent execution by teammates at all levels—even when chaos and uncertainty, such as the loss of key leaders or resources, come into the picture.

- Focus on developing the simplest way of achieving the mission and the commander's intent. For example, don't create a 7-step process when a 4-step process is just as effective—and much easier for everyone to understand and execute with consistency.

- Utilize specific, smart management techniques that simplify things. Examples include clear and succinct communications that rely on a common operating language; the effective use of meetings that have clear agendas, well-structured discussions, and realistic time-frames (such as "60 minutes, max"); and devising templates for complicated projects—such as onboarding the IT components of a newly acquired company—that break down the steps and make priorities and actions easy to understand and execute. There are numerous rules and techniques that can help leaders and their teams simplify all that they do.

It is a leader's duty to introduce and reinforce the concept of simplicity throughout his or her sphere of influence. This habit cuts through the clutter and enables consistency, despite any storm swirling around you and your people. Life and business are complicated enough. Your leadership—including all plans, orders, processes, and communications—shouldn't compound this confusion.

Chapter 32

STANDARD OPERATING PROCEDURES

Despite its reliance on decentralized command and control and developing initiative in individuals, the Marine Corps remains a hierarchical organization with many *very centralized* aspects. The decentralized vs. centralized elements are largely determined by what makes the most sense. While the Marine Corps wants leaders who are free to take initiative on the battlefield, it also needs individual Marines to adhere to established standards for routine tasks that demand consistency and reliability.

To accomplish the latter, the Marine Corps has a seemingly endless number of standard operating procedures (SOPs), for everything from securing a landing zone, to cleaning and maintaining a machine gun, to handling various administrative issues.

The best way to think of well-designed SOPs: they set standards for basic performance that enable delegation and supervision. And when the process, procedures, steps, etc., of administrative and operational tasks are standardized into well-designed SOPs, the resulting efficiency sets individuals free to focus on the things that require creative thinking and innovation.

SOPs can be short, or they can be lengthy. For example, *Marine Corps Artillery Fire Support Training Standing Operating Procedures (SOP)* is a long document that outlines the exact roles, responsibilities, equipment, qualifications, training, and organizational structure of "all fire support teams within [an] artillery regiment."[163]

The artillery training materials get into even more specific SOPs, such as the tactics, techniques, and procedures (TTPs) and essential fire support tasks (EFSTs) for artillery Marines. Take this example of an ESFT for a "deliberate attack;" the standard operating procedure for each one demands outlining a Task, a Purpose, a Method, and the Effects:

- Task: Disrupt the enemy on objective from effectively engaging at-tacking forces with direct fires.

- Purpose: Allow infantry to close and engage the enemy with direct fires.

- Method: Echelon close air support (CAS), artillery and mortar sup-pressive fires across the objective. Priority of fires to TF 2-64, target AD0018, Bn 6 rounds (rds) with marking round and 2 sorties A-10 CAS. airspace coordination area (ACA) Blue in effect.

- Effects: CAS destroys 1 platoon; artillery and mortars provide contin-uous (sustained rate of fire) fires within 200 meters (m) of other 2 platoons until cease or shift fire is ordered.[164]

A great deal of information, common terminology, and other SOPs are packed into that example, enabling the quick execution of a complex task that in-volves very high stakes. To the trained eye, the brief statements contain complex guidance that is easily understood and promotes rapid, coordinated actions of various units participating in a combat operation.

When designed and implemented wisely in any environment, SOPs provide explicit direction, ensure consistency, and increase efficiency. They free up leaders and individual team members to focus their critical thinking skills on problems that are not covered by the procedures. SOPs also contribute to the "common operating language" shared by members of a team. This means that an organization can immediately replace one member with an alternate individual who already knows the role and its actions.

SOPs are Also Vital in the Business World

The best companies, departments, and teams have well-designed SOPs that enable consistent execution of essential tasks.

The distribution arms of successful manufacturers have figured out standard procedures for quickly and economically shipping their products. Human resources departments use SOPs to create a consistent hiring and onboarding experience for new employees. Most successful sales organizations have devised outlines and templates that help their sales reps sell to, upsell, and retain customers.

For example, a salesperson may have a pre-call checklist that involves:

- Researching the prospect

- Setting and sending a meeting agenda

- Gathering supporting materials

- Summarizing key features and benefits of the product or service

- Setting goals

- Summarizing action items after the call

In a decentralized trust-based organization, an individual salesperson will be encouraged to adapt within this framework as various situations require it. But having a checklist like this is a great way to ensure consistent communication, quickly train new sales associates, and ensure that time-tested, successful steps are followed.[165]

When I worked to integrate newly-acquired companies into Kforce, we used a range of SOPs for everything from making initial contact with the leaders of the new company to the content of initial meetings. We also had a checklist of the specific policies, processes, and systems that needed to be addressed to achieve the dates and objectives established by senior executives.

How to Formulate Effective SOPs

SOPs are usually born from experience, and behind many of them lie a problem or even a disaster. Commercial aviation uses countless SOPs, from the preflight checklists for ground crews, pilots, and flight attendants to criteria for grounding aircraft in certain weather conditions—all of which improve safety and efficiency.

In many situations, leaders find that they are having good results in certain areas and they want to reproduce these results at scale. In these cases, they will study the operations that are producing the positive results and reverse-engineer every action from start-to-finish. Once codified into logical sequences and steps, these newly created SOPs are broadcast and continuously emphasized and supervised by the appropriate leaders. In other situations, the need for an effective SOP will stem from mistakes and poor results. They are born from the thought, *Alright, whatever we do, let's make sure we never do **that** again.*

The Three Big Questions

Whether an SOP evolves from a good or a bad experience, it should ideally always come from experience. All good SOPs and, for that matter, all operational activity within an organization should start with the leader asking the *Three Big Questions*:

- What should we start doing?

- What should we stop doing?

- What should we be doing differently?

Note: This highly effective leadership technique—asking the Three Big Questions—will be covered in more detail several times throughout this book.

If you are a leader who is looking to develop a standard operating procedure, creating it closely mirrors how you should execute plans, orders, and other directives. Set the intent and solicit input from key stakeholders; in this case, *the individuals who actually do the task* that an SOP will govern.

An assembly-line manager and his teammates in a manufacturing plant will intuitively know some of the operational inefficiencies that could be eliminated, as well as when suggested procedures will not work. Design your SOPs with input from the front-line executors, with the intent of having them supervised by leaders at that level and perhaps one or two levels above it. If you've developed a trust-based organization with strong values and quality leaders, this input becomes exponentially more precise and actionable.

Walk the Fine Line Between Standardizing and Micromanaging

SOPs can get a bad rap. This usually happens when they are cumbersome or overly precise. When a poorly crafted SOP is put in the hands of a petty or oppressive bureaucrat with little initiative and fewer critical thinking skills, it can tank efficiency and kill morale, as well as common sense.

Relegate SOPs to the things that individuals should not have to think much about, or make them broad enough to be interpreted within the scope of the commander's intent. For example, a specific SOP for a company's preferred method of issuing press releases or other external communications may be as precise as "place the company logo in the upper-right corner of the document, use 12-point Arial font, and employ a standard cover sheet format." It's simple, specific, and easy to implement, and serves to make all written communications look consistent and professional.

In contrast, a good SOP for onboarding a new client may involve weekly follow-up communications that indicate the status of the account for six weeks; initial deliverables provided within two weeks; and scheduling a review meeting with the client at the end of the first month. Again, each SOP should serve to provide a consistent framework to actually speed up operations and make them simpler while ensuring quality results—not slow them down or hamstring initiative.

SOPs Are an Iterative Process

As a leader, it is your responsibility to create and maintain effective SOPs within your sphere of influence. This is once again accomplished by getting feedback from subordinates and front-line executors, who—if you've established a Teacher-Scholar 360° environment—will have the confidence to tell you when something doesn't work.

Leaders may hear teammates make statements like these:

> "I can't get my job done on time because the people ahead of me in the workflow are taking too long."

> "I have to create, read, and sign off on too many reports."

> "Every day, people repeatedly ask me the same questions when they are trying to complete routine tasks."

Comments like these indicate various operational inefficiencies and problems. They may be an indicator of poorly designed SOPs or surface the fact that there are no SOPs at all! Always remember this: If you want to find out which SOPs are not working well, *ask the people who are using them.*

One of your subordinate leaders may tell you, "Look, everybody knows that the SOP for this task says we will do Steps A, B, and C during a certain situation. The truth is that nobody ever does Step B, and this is why…"

This type of input from the front-line executors provides the opportunity to refine the procedure by getting rid of Step B and making other recommended modifications. If you take the time to solicit feedback from your teammates on SOPs and other operational guidelines they are required to use, they will likely say, "Hallelujah!"

The lesson here is that a leader must constantly assess if existing SOPs are effective or not—whether they are actually enabling efficiency and consistency, or they are simply slowing things down, are overly restrictive, or causing other problems.

SOPs Should Set You Free

Again, it is always prudent to create SOPs with input from front-line people. Use them to develop a "common language" of terms and definitions, tactics, techniques, and predetermined actions that increase efficiency and consistency. Tailor them to be broad or specific in relation to the task and the level of initiative and critical thinking it involves.

If they are designed correctly, they will support decentralized leadership in a trust-based organization. SOPs simplify routine tasks and facilitate communication. They also allow individuals to quickly take on new roles and free up your team to spend their time and energy on bigger challenges and new opportunities!

Chapter 33

COMMON OPERATING LANGUAGE

In modern military organizations, the use of standardized terminology and interpretations plays a critical role in various types of activities. This practice enables unit leaders to organize, plan, train, and execute operations using a *common operating language* that is clearly articulated, universally understood, and enforced at all levels. This language helps *simplify* things, as covered in the previous chapter of the book.

Since 1948, military terms have been codified in the Department of Defense Dictionary, and these terms are constantly evaluated for operational relevance and effectiveness; terms are added, deleted, and modified as appropriate. The Marine Corps in particular places great emphasis on the use of a common operating language. The organization leverages definitions and interpretations from this dictionary and other official sources, plus maintains a supplemental Marine Corps-centric dictionary.

These resources enable Marine leaders to effectively plan and execute Maneuver Warfare as well as routine operational and administrative tasks.

Benefits of a Common Language

One of the most significant challenges Marine leaders face during combat operations is the need to quickly assess a situation, make decisions, and direct their unit to adapt to the ever-present *"Fog of War"* on the battlefield. Experience has shown that one of the greatest sources of *internal friction* during situations like this is when various units and individuals use different operational terms and interpretations.

Within a single unit, there may have been several different "dictionaries." As you might expect, this leads to confusion and delayed actions at best—and chaos, failed missions, and unnecessary casualties, at worst. Tragically, in some instances, Marines who were shrouded in the *Fog of War* and confused by the lack of a common operating language unintentionally killed or wounded fellow Marines or noncombatants.

Marine leaders conducted post-operation meetings and after-action reviews in these scenarios, and the lessons led to the use of a common dictionary. The resulting operating language has greatly enhanced the capabilities of Marine combat units.

Application to Business

History has shown the need for a common operating language in companies in any industry and of any size. Most successful companies have created a language that consists of industry- and company-specific terms, definitions, interpretations, and metrics which enable transparency, accountability, and rapid planning and execution. Additionally, the use of a common language helps identify and refine the best practices and standard operating procedures (SOPs) that play a critical role in the Trust-Based Leadership™ model.

This standard communication also influences the establishment and sustainment of a performance-driven culture. When all members of the various divisions, departments and business units speak the same language, great efficiencies are gained in the planning, execution, and supervision of almost any effort.

As an executive leadership coach, many of the clients that I've worked with—both individuals and teams—had not taken the time to establish a common operating language. And some of those who possessed one failed to routinely update and refine it, or enforce its use within their organizations. The results are predictable: precious time is lost as people struggle to interpret what others are saying or requesting.

These challenges and many more can be solved by establishing a common operating language. Identify the routine concepts that are relevant to your operations. Set the terms and definitions. And enforce their use to drive clear communication and smart standard operating procedures.

Chapter 34

FRICTION

Legendary Prussian general and military strategist Carl von Clausewitz used the term "friction" to describe the innumerable, random factors—everything from inclement weather to personality conflicts—that distinguish "real war from war on paper." He described it as "the force that makes the apparently easy so difficult."

MCDP (Marine Corps Doctrinal Publication) 1: Warfighting addresses friction, as it did when it was originally published as *Fleet Marine Force Manual (FMFM) 1* in 1989. *Warfighting* was "drafted by Captain John Schmitt under the direction of the USMC Commandant, General Alfred M. Gray," and both cited ancient Chinese military strategist Sun Tzu as their main inspiration—but there is clearly a lot of Clausewitz in there:[166]

> Friction is the force that resists all action and saps energy. It makes the simple difficult and the difficult seemingly impossible. ...
>
> Friction may be mental, as in indecision over a course of action. It may be physical, as in effective enemy fire or a terrain obstacle that must be overcome. Friction may be external, imposed by enemy action, the terrain, weather, or mere chance. Friction may be self-induced, caused by such factors as lack of a clearly defined goal, lack of coordination, unclear or

complicated plans, complex task organizations or command relationships, or complicated technologies. Whatever form it takes, because war is a human enterprise, friction will always have a psychological as well as a physical impact.

While we should attempt to minimize self-induced friction, the greater requirement is to fight effectively despite the existence of friction. One essential means to overcome friction is the will; we prevail over friction through persistent strength of mind and spirit.[167]

The presence of friction is inevitable in combat and a Marine leader must be able to account for and deal with it. But any leader, including those in the business world, will encounter friction. A sudden loss of resources. A lack of time to get something critical done. A failure by a critical supplier or some other random event that threatens a project. Business leaders must remain composed and propel the organization forward, despite any challenges.

As in warfare, every industry, profession, company, or team encounters two main types of friction:

External Friction

These are things you have little control over that arise from outside of the organization. In combat, it could be the presence of a much bigger enemy force than anticipated or inclement weather that prevents close air support from helping ground forces. Examples in business might be a broad economic crash, the unexpected loss of a critical supplier of raw materials, or even a natural disaster or a fire at a facility which disrupts operations. Leaders may not be able to control whether or not external friction happens, but they can certainly control how they react to it with proper planning and the establishment of effective standard operating procedures (SOPs).

Internal Friction

Sometimes referred to as "self-imposed friction," internal friction includes unplanned challenges and situations that happen within the organization, such as a key team member getting sick or leaving for another job, or a critical IT system going down. In some cases, a leader can influence and minimize the occurrence of internal friction. In other instances, he or she cannot.

During military operations or an intense period in a business, internal friction may be self-imposed, such as when a leader is unable (or unwilling) to decide which course of action to take or otherwise reacts too slowly to rapidly changing circumstances. Internal friction can be the result of defective leadership, personality clashes among team members, poor coordination or communication, inadequate planning or training, lack of mental or physical preparation, or many other things that are generally controllable, to some extent.

In other words, the way to reduce these internal sources of friction is to lead your organization well and create an environment in which the possibility of friction is minimized—and when it happens, quickly addressed and rectified. There is no substitute for engaged leadership in situations like these. In most instances, any type of internal friction can be quickly eliminated or minimized by isolating the sources of "friction points" and properly addressing them.

How you respond to and overcome challenges is key to leading well in an adaptive organization. And this maxim applies to both types of friction.

Dealing with Friction in the Trust-Based Leadership™ Model

The Trust-Based Leadership™ model assumes that there will be friction during all types of business operations—and many of its concepts and techniques are specifically designed to help leaders deal with it.

If you can effectively implement all or most pieces of the Trust-Based Leadership model within your team, you'll directly and indirectly reduce the existence of friction, especially the type that stems from the organization itself. The following techniques help a leader specifically mitigate internal, *self-imposed* friction while making his or her team better equipped to deal with *all* types of friction:

- **Mission-type orders with clear commander's intent minimize friction.** Trusted subordinates who are empowered to take initiative have the latitude to deal with unexpected events. They can either propose solutions when problems with the initial plan or existing SOPs surface or, when appropriate, simply adapt to the situation and take immediate action to remedy it.

In many instances, some of this friction may not ever even come to a more-senior leader's attention, because her empowered subordinate leaders have been trained to have a bias for action and to exercise initiative in the pursuit of achieving the commander's intent. And remember, simplicity, brevity, and clarity in orders, communications, and plans make mission-type orders possible.

- **Standard Operating Procedures (SOPs) and detailed planning can minimize friction.** Marine leaders can't exactly predict what the enemy's going to do in a given situation, but they can account for internal factors with relative certainty. For example, a leader knows what kind of ammunition his Marines need to carry and in what quantities as well as what the resupply methods are, even during an active combat action.

  There are SOPs for executing this resupply and countless other activities, such as calling in air strikes or artillery support, evacuating casualties, linking-up with an adjacent unit, and even communicating if radios are suddenly rendered ineffective due to technical problems or enemy electronic countermeasures.

  All of these scenarios create significant amounts of friction. Having effective SOPs can help minimize it to manageable levels.

- **Having a clear core focus minimizes friction.** In the Marine Corps, this core focus is winning battles. When this couples with mission-type orders, both elements serve as a compass to guide decisions at all levels during challenging times.

- **Core values and a strong culture minimize friction.** A culture of integrity, execution, and excellence ensures that a team will rise to meet challenges, rather than procrastinate, evade responsibility, or fold under pressure.

- **Train like you fight.** Proper training that replicates some of the impact of friction is incredibly valuable in combat, and it also has importance in the business world. While it's impossible to exactly replicate real-world combat conditions, great training serves to prepare Marines for the stress and uncertainty that arise from friction.

Business leaders have an advantage here because their teams are operating daily in the *real-world* conditions of their industry, company, department, or team. The opportunity to observe and evaluate the performance of your teammates as they conduct business operations is something that should be exploited. This evaluation serves as the basis for continuous improvement in all aspects of employees' roles and responsibilities.

All of the above elements particularly minimize **self-imposed** friction. Some companies wonder why their team members suddenly leave for other jobs, and perhaps why they have such a high overall rate of turnover. Others don't understand why they continually miss deadlines or often roll out failed products or services. Avoidable friction is often the culprit.

An effective trust-based organization is not only better at dealing with external or unexpected internal friction—it naturally minimizes the *self-imposed* variety that stresses people out and causes inefficiencies or failure. Employees who are fairly compensated, trained and developed professionally, and given clear standards and the necessary autonomy to do their jobs don't tend to leave suddenly.

Mitigating Internal Friction Frees Up Resources to Tackle External Friction

Think of a simple Marine Corps analogy: A Marine unit is located in a forward operating base in Afghanistan and told to be ready to execute offensive operations within an hour of being notified of a mission. The unit commander and his staff will ensure that all administrative, logistical, and operations details have been worked out, with appropriate back-ups and contingency plans in place. The unit has trusted, well-trained leaders at every level and the unit's pre-deployment training, existing SOPs, mission-type orders, and other trust-based elements make it as ready as possible to successfully execute difficult missions on short notice.

In this example, the combined impact of effective leadership and the best-practices of a trust-based organization have greatly minimized potential sources of internal friction or even eliminated them from the equation. Because the unit leader has taken steps to ensure that his team is in a high-state of readiness, the unit will have more "gas in the tank" to use when executing complex, dangerous missions on short notice. And they'll better handle the various forms of *external* friction that *always* appear during combat operations.

As you already know, this unit commander and his Marines are simply applying and executing the concepts and techniques of traditional Marine Corps leadership and Maneuver Warfare. And the Trust-Based Leadership model that I teach to business leaders looks very much like this when its applied to companies of all sizes, within any industry.

External Friction Tends to Come in Waves—Reverse the Momentum

Sources of internal friction sometimes overlap with a period of intense external friction, such as the loss of a major client, an economic collapse, or the sudden emergence of a "disruptor" like Uber, Airbnb, or SpaceX in an industry or business niche. If you haven't built an organization that minimizes internal friction and can effectively handle external sources of it, your company could be swamped by waves of intense friction.

I spoke to a very experienced member of a Marine Corps special operations unit about the effects of friction during combat operations and asked him to provide some of his thoughts on the topic. He had this to say:

> Your examples of internal and external friction are spot-on; both types of friction can be found in almost everything my unit does, whether it is during training or while on real-world ops. Our experience has enabled us, through honest and detailed self-assessment of our team members and our actions, to pinpoint most of the areas in which internal friction can exist.
>
> To be honest, we found that most of our internal friction issues were associated with personality clashes and inadequate communication between the unit leaders and the guys at the tip of the spear, so to speak. We've done a lot of work to ensure that our leaders and team members are on the same frequency regarding the objectives and plan of attack throughout all phases of an operation. We have done a lot to eliminate the inevitable personality clashes that can arise when you have so many strong-willed, high-achieving, "Type-A" personalities operating with each other.
>
> If you look at various professional sports teams, many of them seem to be dominated by or overly focused on the personality

or talent of one or perhaps just a few of the players. And many of these teams end up having problems due to this. In our unit, we do our best to eliminate the "prima donna" or "superstar" mentality that might exist; it simply isn't tolerated.

When it comes to external friction, we've just come to accept that it will exist despite our best intelligence and planning efforts, and that like any other combat unit, our success will always depend on our operators being able to think on their feet and make the right decisions when things happen that make our game plan unworkable.

To sum it up, we do everything possible from an individual and unit perspective to minimize instances of internal friction, and we train relentlessly to enhance our ability to successfully cope with every imaginable type of external friction.[168]

Don't minimize the psychological impact of friction. To continue the above sports analogy, you often see a team that has lost momentum get rolled over by their opponents. The losing players are put on their heels and play reactively and ineffectively. A leader must understand that when enough friction occurs, it can send you or your team into a spiral of doubt, frustration, and confusion.

How you react as a leader to external friction—ideally, with decisiveness and poise—will help set the tone for your team and prevent this losing spiral. You may not be able to control external friction, but if you accept and meet it head on, you are more likely to prevent it from devolving into something that's even more negative. Also, be sure to support members of your team who have a harder time dealing with friction. Firm leadership and a helping hand can go a long way toward completely shifting someone's outlook. They are incredibly powerful tools.

Good leaders expect to experience friction and develop the focus, poise, and mindset to deal with it. They set up the trust-based elements necessary to minimize internal friction and contingency plan for sources of external friction that are reasonable possibilities. Otherwise, they quickly, confidently, and decisively adapt to the unexpected.

Focus your energy and effort on the things you can control (internal friction), and don't waste much time worrying about the things that you can't (most sources of external friction). When those bad things happen—and they will—don't get consumed by stress or inaction. If you're a real leader, you know it's simply part of the job!

"There are two types of friction. The best leaders know how to adapt to the first and minimize the second."

—Mike Ettore

Chapter 35

DETACHMENT

In addition to "friction" (and many other brilliant military observations), Prussian general and military strategist Carl von Clausewitz wrote about a concept that led to the commonly used phrase *"the fog of war"* which describes confusion in battle:

> "War is the realm of uncertainty; three quarters of the factors on which action in war is based are wrapped in a fog of greater or lesser uncertainty. A sensitive and discriminating judgement is called for; a skilled intelligence to scent out the truth."[169]

Combat is perhaps the ultimate stressful activity. When you combine that intense stress with confusion, randomness, and complexity, clear judgement is often a casualty. This is why combat leaders must learn to mentally detach and literally or figuratively *"step outside of the firefight"* to gather their thoughts and gain perspective on the situation they are dealing with.

Detaching to Achieve Clarity

Picture a Marine company commander or platoon commander leading a combat operation in an urban environment. He may be situated on the rooftop of a building 30 meters or more to the rear of his lead elements that are actively engaged in a firefight. This somewhat detached position enables him to see things that the Marines who are fully engaged in intense combat can't see, plus it removes some of the intense stress of direct combat from his decision-making process.

"From my elevated vantage point, I can see three enemy armored vehicles coming down an adjacent street. My Marines on the ground can't see them. I'm directing them to change their location so they can protect their exposed flank and I am calling in close air support on the enemy vehicles."

Call it detachment, reflection, gaining perspective, or something else, but leaders of all types must often remove themselves, even if only slightly, from the chaos, pressure, and tunnel vision of a situation to make the right decision. The sayings *"can't see the forest for the trees"* and *"you can't view the picture if you're inside the frame"* are good descriptions of this concept.

Gaining Perspective and Clarity Apply in Any Complicated Situation

In the above example, having less immediate fear of getting killed has obvious value for the combat leader. But the benefits of *stepping outside of the firefight* can apply to any leader who must make a difficult decision or assess a complicated situation.

Removing yourself from the stress of a *business "*firefight," if it's feasible and realistic, can result in better analysis and decision-making. Of course, some stress can be a good thing, physiologically-speaking:

> A moderate increase in heart rate can improve performance because it increases the amount of blood in the brain, and the neurotransmitter activity that enhances cognitive processing, according to Lee Waller, director of research at the UK's Hult International Business School.
>
> "We think clearly, make good decisions and learn well," she says. But too much stress causes the opposite response as more blood flows to the limbs—known as "fight or flight" and that reduces cognitive function.[170]

Intense stress—and too much of it, for too long—has a variety of negative short- and long-term effects on an individual. Scientists have conducted numerous studies that outline the impact of stress on decision-making. Much of this research involves rats, not humans—but it has still led to interesting insights. (Plus, there's probably a great rat-race metaphor for these studies.)

One neuroscientist from the University of Washington drew this conclusion from his study:

> "The stressed animals took longer to learn and weren't adjusting their behavior in the maze," said Jones. "From this research we can see the effects of stress on rats and how one episode of stress impairs their decision making for several days.
>
> We know humans have to make numerous higher-level decisions, some of which are complex and require deliberations. Rats are guided by survival, and seeking out the larger of two rewards for the same effort should be fundamentally easy. The fact that stress can have such an effect on a simple but critical task is amazing."[171]

And long-term stress has been tied (in humans, this time) to both impaired decision-making as well as lasting brain changes, including dementia.[172]

As a leader, briefly removing stress during intense situations can help you make much better decisions. And making a practice of identifying and mitigating *ongoing* forms of stress—including through coping techniques that help you frame it differently—will benefit both your health and durability as a leader.

Time and Space = Opportunity for Reflection and Gaining Perspective

As a business leader, sometimes it's best to force yourself to take a break, go grab a cup of coffee, or take a short walk outside. These are simple ways to make it a practice to step outside of "business firefights," when you have the opportunity to do so.

Leave your office or the conference room, politely step away from people talking to you, and get into an environment in which you can think clearly. Deliberately consider scenarios or potential solutions to a problem that may not otherwise occur to you when you are sitting in a meeting. If the situation allows for it, don't be afraid to tell the members of your staff, "Let me sleep on this tonight. I'll have some thoughts and recommendations to share with you tomorrow morning."

When I was making non-combat decisions in the Marine Corps, I would sometimes tell my subordinate leaders, "Okay, I got it. Is there any more information that anyone wants to give me before I go have a cup of coffee and think this over?" Often, I'd go out for a run and mull over the situation while I exercised. Some of the very best decisions I've ever made were the result of reflection while conducting physical exercise, and I know many leaders who've had similar success doing this to step outside of "firefights." As a business leader, I'd often leave my office and take a drive or head to a local Starbucks to get some alone time with my thoughts.

In either scenario, several things would happen: I'd usually think about some important questions that I had forgotten to ask my colleagues during a recent meeting on the challenge we were facing. By stepping away and putting myself in an environment in which "I could hear myself think," I could view the specific scenario or problem from a different angle. And often, potential solutions would suddenly present themselves, clear as day.

I'm not telling you anything novel; we've all done this. What is relevant to your development as a leader is the fact that <u>you have to train yourself to do this when it's appropriate</u>. Don't routinely get so sucked into situations that you forget to "step outside of the firefight" to gather your thoughts and gain perspective. Learn to consciously decide to "take yourself out of the picture frame" when necessary.

Enlist Others to Gain Perspective

Stepping outside of the firefight doesn't always involve thinking about a scenario on your own, especially when you are so close to a problem that truly independent or unbiased thinking is difficult to do. This is one of the biggest benefits of cultivating a team of great mentors, trusted colleagues, and friends. If there is someone whom you respect and is more detached from an issue than you are, he or she may be able to provide you with some surprising insights. Tap into these resources routinely—you'll be better off if you do!

Also, work to develop the practice of detachment in your subordinate leaders. Everyone can benefit from this technique when formulating plans or making complex decisions, including leaders at every level of any organization. Encourage them to mentally detach when the situation allows for it. Many of my junior leaders in the Marine Corps quickly learned the value of stepping outside of the firefight, either naturally or through my emphasis on them doing it.

And at times, my leaders felt the best thing to do was to detach *me* from a situation so they could reflect and gain perspective on an issue. The words "time for a cup of coffee" were often the code for "please leave us alone for a while, sir" in these situations.

"Sir, this might be a good time for you to go get a cup of coffee. When you get back, we'll have some recommended courses of actions ready for your review."

My absence enabled my leaders to discuss issues and potential solutions without their commander hovering over their shoulder. As a senior executive, I would also often ask my leaders:

"Is this a good time for me to go get a cup of coffee?"

"Yes, it is, Mike. In fact, have two cups and come back in a couple of hours. We'll have some options ready to discuss with you."

Mentorship Includes Kicking Back Plans to See if They Can Be Improved

Not only would I teach my subordinate leaders that they should look at an issue from another angle, I often *insisted* on it. While this practice can be abused, applying it judiciously can vastly improve decisions and plans.

When approached with an issue on Monday morning, I'd ask them, "When do we have to make this decision?"

"Friday."

"Okay. How about this? Each of you step away and think about this situation by yourselves for the rest of the day and evening. Then, get together tomorrow, brainstorm it as a team, and come back to me Wednesday morning with some options based upon your collective wisdom and expertise."

Nearly every time my leaders brought me options based upon their combined efforts, they were better than any I would have produced on my own—even though in many instances, my experience was far greater than theirs. Likewise, the options they arrived at by collaborating with each other were almost always better than they would have produced individually. The lesson here is that—if time permits—it is almost always better to <u>leverage the experience and ingenuity of your teammates to solve problems!</u>

Stepping Outside of the Firefight Requires Judgement and Balance

A leader who steps out for a break before *every* decision is indecisive and ineffective. One who *never* does it may be impulsive and equally ineffective. Pick and choose when you need some time to detach from your surroundings. Do it when you know you have the time *and* that inner voice tells you that a quick decision may be an inferior one.

Marine combat leaders often literally "step outside of a firefight" to make decisions, but many times, they don't have the luxury. The ability to function under fire is essential in a combat leader. Fortunately, the business world affords many more opportunities for reflection. We're not typically being shot at, though it may feel like it at times!

The vast majority of business decisions afford the time to think and reflect, especially more-complex scenarios that have naturally longer timelines. Sometimes, just a night's rest will give you an entirely different perspective and, in some instances, issues may actually resolve themselves or new opportunities could arise before taking a course of action.

In my experience, business leadership is almost always the direct opposite of combat leadership in this regard. There is a time and a place for instantaneous decision-making in business, but in most scenarios, there's usually more time to consider various options and courses of action. A lot more time. Don't rush to make a decision today that must be made three days from now, unless you're absolutely confident you've got all of the information, it's not going to change, and moving now is going to help your team have more time to plan out the execution.

I'm a very Type-A personality, and as such, I tend to be very decisive. I'm the type of person who is always looking for problems that I can help other leaders solve. I want to lead and help my teammates achieve their goals and objectives! Those are generally good qualities in a leader, but they can also be flaws. In the business world, I eventually learned to tell myself:

> "Mike, this isn't combat. You don't need to decide everything right now. In fact, you don't need to decide everything at all. You have a lot of smart people on your team—give them some room to run!"

I wish I'd learned this earlier!

Chapter 36

THE FORCE MULTIPLIER

The Trust-Based Leadership™ model helps create adaptive, powerful organizations that can succeed in dynamic and often chaotic environments. These organizations are resilient and durable—they can take a hit and keep functioning despite unforeseen challenges and even the loss of key leaders.

Once again, think of all of the elements that make up a trust-based organization:

- A strong culture, a core focus, and core values which shape all teammates into a tight, unified team that executes with excellence.

- The training and development of leaders at all levels, with a focus on integrity, mission accomplishment, accountability, responsibility, delegation, and effective supervision.

- A decentralized command and control (C2) model that includes:

    o Mission-type orders that enable individuals to execute them with initiative.

    o Simple, clear plans, orders, and communications.

    o Standard operating procedures that increase efficiency and free up individuals up to innovate in other areas.

- Personal and organizational strategies that minimize internal friction and prepare for external friction.

- Leaders who know the value of *stepping outside of the fire-fight* to reflect and gain perspective.

I've told you that the Trust-Based Leadership™ model is being leveraged by many successful organizations. But by now, you may wonder, "Ok, you've said it's great. But what makes it *better* than some other models? What's the *secret sauce* of Trust-Based Leadership?"

The main reason for the success of the Trust-Based Leadership model is a senior leader's ability to *delegate to and leverage* the experience, ingenuity, and initiative of a highly trained and capable multi-level leadership team.

The Force Multiplier

The Marine Corps places a lot of faith in its junior officers and non-commissioned officers (both *staff* non-commissioned officers (SNCOs) and regular NCOs), and in many ways, they are the engine that powers the institution. Newly commissioned lieutenants are taught, "Listen to your SNCOs and NCOs. Learn to delegate effectively and leverage their experience and wisdom." In turn, the SNCOs and NCOs are told, "Teach and develop your young officers. Show them that you're worthy of their respect and confidence in you."

As a Marine leader, I invested in and relied on *all* of my leaders, not just my officers and SNCOs, as some other commanders tended to do. Of course, I greatly leveraged the more-senior leaders, but I also bet heavily on the many sergeants and corporals within the unit. Throughout my entire Marine Corps career, I ensured that my *entire* leadership team—all officers, SNCOs, and NCOs—were completely aligned on the most important concepts and operational priorities. A leadership team that is in sync to this degree is a very powerful force that is capable of delivering amazing results!

This synchronization can also be successfully utilized in the business world. I've done it—repeatedly and at every level of leadership—within a large, publicly traded company. Even better, I have taught many other leaders to do it. They soon realized that the most effective way to ensure organizational success is by continuously developing *other* leaders and forging them into a cohesive and focused leadership *team*.

I've said it before about applying Marine Corps leadership concepts to the business world, and I'll say it again: <u>this stuff really works!</u>

Leadership Team > Senior Leaders

In my experience, leadership training and the expectation of leadership competence at all levels are far less common in the business world than they are in the Marine Corps. The concept of executives ensuring that their "junior officers, SNCOs, and NCOs" are being developed as a unified, fully aligned leadership team is foreign to the vast majority of organizations.

Instead, a lot of emphasis is placed solely on executives. Essentially, the company "bets on the senior leaders" to get things done. Trusting these executives isn't always a bad thing, as long as those senior leaders have other strong leaders within their teams who are capable of executing and supervising plans and operations.

But sadly, in too many organizations, the reliance on senior leadership results in a failure to invest in the development of more-junior leaders. These individuals are often expected to succeed with minimal, if any, leadership training, coaching, and mentoring.

The solution to this problem: Getting senior leaders to understand that one of their main responsibilities is to *develop* current and future leaders.

Junior Officers, SNCOs, and NCOs = Directors, Managers, Supervisors, and Team Leaders

The titles of leaders may vary from one company to another, but as you read this chapter, I am sure you'll be able to figure out who the junior officers, SNCOs, and NCOs are in your organization. Make it a priority to develop them to the point that you can rely on them to consistently produce outstanding results with minimal guidance and supervision. The critical point is that <u>you must focus on continuously training and developing leaders at every level</u>. This conscious and consistent effort is needed to forge them into a fully aligned and highly capable leadership team.

To do this, you must become comfortable delegating your authority in various ways to your leaders, while effectively supervising them as they execute orders. Unless you're Einstein, Superman, or some combination of the two, at some point, you aren't going to be able to do it all yourself. You may do things as well as you can, but you'll never match the combined mental and operational horsepower resident in your leadership team.

The Flagpole Lesson Applies in the Business World

We've previously mentioned the flagpole example; an instructional exercise in which new Marine lieutenants are taught the importance of delegation and leverage. Let's go over it again:

> A Marine instructor presents a class of newly commissioned second lieutenants with a scenario:
>
> "You are told by your company commander on Monday morning, 'Lieutenant, you see the flagpole next to the parade deck? We need to take it down and put the new one up. We need it done by 1700 on Saturday; we're going to have a battalion change of command ceremony at that time. This is your mission. Get it done.'"
>
> The instructor provides a list of the dozen or so Marines under each new lieutenant's command and their ranks—including a gunnery sergeant, who is the lieutenant's direct report—and also provides "a detailed list of materials and equipment," and gives the class 30 minutes to individually plan and write down their orders. Some of the new lieutenants create incredibly detailed schemes and step-by-step orders; invariably, most of the class tries to ace the test by writing orders that are complex. It was a trick question, of course.[173]
>
> At the end of the lesson, the instructor collects the orders and tells the students the correct answer:
>
> "Lieutenants, this is what you should do in this situation. Approach the gunnery sergeant and tell him, 'Gunny, the Captain just told me that we need to have the new flagpole installed by 1700 on Saturday for the battalion change of command ceremony. Let's meet again later this afternoon so you can brief me on your plan and discuss any resources and support you will need. Once the plan is approved, you can assemble the Marines and begin the work. I'll meet with you early each morning and late each afternoon to discuss the

project's progress and to provide any support you may need from me. I'll also visit the work area a few times each day to see how things are going and to talk with the Marines.'"

As the senior leader in charge, the young (and inexperienced) lieutenant approves the plan, he knows that he must supervise it well by applying the *S in BAMCIS*, and that he alone is responsible if the new flagpole fails to go up on time—but he's delegated to the Gunny the appropriate level of authority required to accomplish the mission, and then stepped back to allow the Gunny and his Marines the freedom to operate without being micro-managed.

This simple lesson can also help business leaders understand that delegation should be a "default setting." And to do this, they must prioritize the growth of their team's *other* leaders.

A trust-based organization that's *firing on all cylinders* develops and fully leverages leaders at all levels, from senior executives down to front-line managers and supervisors. If a leader can get these individuals unified and focused on achieving the mission and intent, the organization becomes exponentially more powerful.

My time in the "leadership trenches" (that has imparted a few tough lessons along the way!) showed me that my teams were *always* more successful when I bet on all leaders—and when I made it clear to senior leaders *that one of their main responsibilities was the development of other leaders.*

When leaders are nurtured and all of their efforts are synchronized, these individuals become a team—one that's an exponential, virtually unstoppable force-multiplier.

Section II

SUMMARY

Let's go over what we've just learned.

I've explained why **Trust** is essential to how the Marine Corps functions, as well as the Trust-Based Leadership™ model that's based on Marine leadership concepts and my experience as a military and civilian leader.

You've learned how **Mission Tactics**, **Mission-Type Orders**, and **Commander's Intent** rely on and develop this trust by leveraging competent leaders and teammates at all levels. These elements enable **Decentralized Command and Control (C2)** in the military and in business. And decentralized organizations tend to run rings around rigidly centralized ones—seizing opportunities faster, making better decisions, and adapting more quickly to new challenges.

I've explained how Trust-Based leaders must be able to adapt **Priority of Effort** in the face of rapidly changing conditions and keep all things—plans, communications, orders, processes, and more—**Simple**, to the extent possible. Well-designed **Standard Operating Procedures (SOPs)** and a **Common Operating Language** enable this simplicity, as well as the efficiency and consistent execution that free up teams to spend their energy on tasks that require innovation and critical thinking.

You've learned what **Friction** (internal or self-imposed, as well as external) is, why it is often inevitable, and how to deal with it. I've explained how minimizing the former gives you resources to tackle the latter; plus how

Detachment that achieves clarity ("stepping outside of the firefight") enables better decisions.

And finally, I've revealed one of the "secret weapons" of leadership: Why leveraging leaders at all levels is **The Force Multiplier** that unleashes the true power of any unit, department, or organization.

These are the main components of the Trust-Based Leadership model. You've got the basic blueprint. But just like the Marine Corps needs certain types of leaders to execute maneuver warfare doctrine, so are leaders with specific traits required to make Trust-Based Leadership work.

That's where this next section comes in. I will explain the key characteristics, skills, and attitudes of Trust-Based leaders while encouraging you to develop these elements in yourself.

As you read this section, keep the following in mind: While these traits are essential for operating in a Trust-Based Leadership™ model, know that they will also serve you well as a leader in *any* organization or situation. If you diligently focus on developing and applying them, you will undoubtedly go far in leadership, business, and life.

Let's dive in.

"I've found that the very best leaders in Corporate America almost all practice some of the Trust-Based Leadership™ concepts and principles that I experienced in the Marine Corps and teach to clients. That said, the *majority* of business leaders I encounter do not approach leadership from the perspective of trust.

Ultimately, my discussions with the '*non-trusters*' lead to the fact that they have been 'burned' or 'stabbed in the back' in the past, and this has soured them on the idea of empowering and trusting their peers and teammates. Some of these leaders muster the courage required to 'trust again' but some cannot bring themselves to do it, fearing poor results or even betrayal at the hands of their colleagues.

I applaud those in the former group and feel genuine sadness for the latter—knowing that without the ability to trust others, it's unlikely that they will ever attain their maximum potential or that of the teams they lead."

—Mike Ettore

Bonus Resources

Download Your Bonus Resources!

The graphics used in *Principles of War for the Corporate Battlefield* and *Trust-Based Leadership*™ and additional resources are available for free in the Bonus Resource Vault, which you can find at:

HTTPS://FIDELISLEADERSHIP.COM/BOOKBONUS

Social Media – Let's Stay In Touch!

Fidelis Leadership Podcast: https://www.fidelisleadership.com/podcast

Facebook
- Fidelis: www.facebook.com/FidelisLeadershipGroup
- Mike: www.facebook.com/EttoreMike

Linkedin:
- Fidelis: www.linkedin.com/company/fidelis-leadership-group-llc
- Mike: www.linkedin.com/in/mikeettore/

Twitter: https://twitter.com/FidelisLeader

Instagram: www.instagram.com/fidelisleadership/

Fidelis Leadership Newsletter

Receive monthly emails containing valuable lessons, tactics and techniques that can help you become a World-Class Leader! I promise that I will never share your contact information in any way, and if you decide to stop receiving the newsletter you can unsubscribe with one click.

SIGN UP NOW! HTTPS://FIDELISLEADERSHIP.COM

"A PLACE OF LEARNING FOR THOSE ASPIRING TO LEADERSHIP EXCELLENCE!"

The Fidelis Leadership Podcast is for those who want to become World Class Leaders. Weekly episodes convey lessons and advice from some of the world's foremost leadership experts, and discussions regarding the effective application of the Trust-Based Leadership™ model.

HTTPS://WWW.FIDELISLEADERSHIP.COM/PODCAST

Also Found on Your Favorite Podcast Platforms!

From the Author

Book Reviews

Thank you for reading my book. Please consider visiting the site where you purchased it and writing a brief review. Your feedback is important to me and will help others decide whether to read the book too.

New Books, Training Programs and Events

If you'd like to get notifications of my latest books, training programs and leadership events, please join my email list by visiting https://fidelisleadership.com

Bulk Purchase Discounts

If you would like to purchase 25 or more print copies of this book, we are happy to offer you a discount on the net list price of the book. Please send inquiries to: info@fidelisleadership.com

Fidelis Leadership Group
Developing World Class Leaders

My Services

Executive Coaching

My executive coaching engagements are uniquely tailored to each individual and are designed to provide focus that can deepen an executive's self-awareness and promote personal and professional growth. The private coaching sessions provide leaders with an opportunity to engage in focused, constructive, and confidential dialogue with a skilled and objective listener. I collaborate with each leader to design a program that fosters and accelerates individual growth, while providing the coaching and facilitation to achieve desired outcomes.

Leadership Development

I help educate, train, and coach leaders so they can dramatically accelerate their personal and professional development. I work best with clients who operate in a culture of execution, accountability, and leadership by example—or those who desire to create such a culture within their organizations. I offer customized leadership training and development programs - including onsite training seminars - for leaders at every level: C-Suite and SVP-VP-Director level, high-potential individuals and others serving in mid-level and front-line leadership roles.

Speaking

I am an experienced public speaker with a strong history of delivering dynamic, interactive, and memorable presentations and keynote speeches to a wide range of organizations. Leveraging leadership lessons that were forged in the unforgiving crucible of combat and while serving as a senior executive, I inspire and energize my audiences and provide them with actionable strategies, tactics, and techniques that they can implement immediately upon returning to their teams.

CONTACT ME NOW!
info@fidelisleadership.com
813-699-3023

Notes and Sources

ENDNOTES

Introduction

1   Pietersen, Willie. "Von Clausewitz on War: Six Lessons for the Modern Strategist." *Ideas and Insights*. Columbia Business School. https://www8.gsb.columbia.edu/articles/node/1788/von-clausewitz-on-war-six-lessons-for-the-modern-strategist

2   Greenberg, Susan H. "Gil-li Vardi: Can Businesses Learn from Military Strategy?" *Insights by Stanford Business*. Stanford Graduate School of Business. https://www.gsb.stanford.edu/insights/gil-li-vardi-can-businesses-learn-military-strategy

3   Malhotra, Deepak. "War and Peace: The Lessons of History for Leadership, Strategy, Negotiation, Policy and Humanity." Harvard Business School. https://www.hbs.edu/course-catalog/2295.html

4   Markides, Constantinos C. *Game-Changing Strategies: How to Create New Market Space in Established Industries by Breaking the Rules*. Jossey-Bass. 2008. https://books.google.com/books?id=I1CVd09Hh7YC&pg=PT117&lpg=PT117&dq=canon+%22beat+xerox-%22&source=bl&ots=ocjY6A8Yvl&sig=ACfU3U1aIcSYlswurkCYBCFBMls9X5U5_g&hl=en&sa=X-&ved=2ahUKEwixi97nsNHoAhWwct8KHZWCBmUQ6AEwBHoECAwQNw#v=onepage&q=canon%20%22beat%20xerox%22&f=false

5   Stacey, Ralph D. *Managing the Unknowable: Strategic Boundaries Between Order and Chaos in Organizations*. Jossey-Bass. 1992. p. 140.

6   Little, Becky. "How the 'Blood Feud' Between Coke and Pepsi Escalated During the 1980s Cola Wars." History.com. https://www.history.com/news/cola-wars-pepsi-new-coke-failure

7   Fuller, John Frederick Charles. *The Foundations of the Science of War*. London: Hutchinson & Co. 1926

8   Ettrich, Brian B. "The Principles of War: Are They Still Applicable?" Naval Postgraduate School. June 2005. https://apps.dtic.mil/sti/pdfs/ADA435689.pdf

9   *U.S. Army Field Manual FM-3 Operations*. Headquarters. Department of the Army. Pg. A-1–A-3.

10   "Operation Desert Storm." GlobalSecurity.org. https://www.globalsecurity.org/military/ops/desert_storm.htm

11   "Coca-Cola Company Statistics and Facts." market.us. https://market.us/statistics/food-and-beverage-companies/coca-cola-company/

12   "Annual Results." Michelin. https://www.michelin.com/en/finance/results-and-presentations/annual-results/

1. Objective

13   "Operation Desert Shield." GlobalSecurity.org. https://www.globalsecurity.org/military/ops/desert_shield.htm

14   "Operation Desert Storm." GlobalSecurity.org. https://www.globalsecurity.org/military/ops/desert_storm.htm

15   "TACTICAL FUNDAMENTALS B2B2269 STUDENT HANDOUT." United States Marine Corps. Basic Officer Course. The Basic School. Pg. 7

16   Greenberg, Julia. "Once Upon a Time, Yahoo Was the Most Important Internet Company." *Wired*. https://www.wired.com/2015/11/once-upon-a-time-yahoo-was-the-most-important-internet-company/

17   Saurel, Sylvain. "6 Reasons Why Yahoo! Failed." *Medium*. https://medium.com/swlh/6-reasons-why-yahoo-failed-6004d67e86ff

18   Greenberg, Julia. "Once Upon a Time, Yahoo Was the Most Important Internet Company." *Wired*. https://www.wired.com/2015/11/once-upon-a-time-yahoo-was-the-most-important-internet-company/

19   "List of mergers and acquisitions by Yahoo!" Wikipedia. https://en.wikipedia.org/wiki/List_of_mergers_and_acquisitions_by_Yahoo!

20   Saurel, Sylvain. "6 Reasons Why Yahoo! Failed." *Medium*. https://medium.com/swlh/6-reasons-why-yahoo-failed-6004d67e86ff

21   Larson, Selena. "Every single Yahoo account was hacked - 3 billion in all." CNN Business. https://money.cnn.com/2017/10/03/technology/business/yahoo-breach-3-billion-accounts/index.html

22   Malone, Michael S. "The UnGoogle (Yes, Yahoo!)." *Wired*. https://www.wired.com/2005/03/yahoo/

23   "Warby Parker Impact Report 2018." https://www.warbyparker.com/assets/img/impact-report/report-2018.pdf

24   Eng, Dinah. "In Hindsight: How Warby Parker Got Its Start." *Fortune*. https://fortune.com/2019/05/30/warby-parker-founders/

25   Clement, J. "Paypal's net revenue from 1st quarter 2010 to 4th quarter 2019." Statista. https://www.statista.com/statistics/218517/paypals-net-revenue-per-quarter/

26   PayPal editorial staff. "How PayPal credit card processing works for your business." PayPal. https://www.paypal.com/us/brc/article/how-paypal-works-for-sellers

27   Furr, Nathan and Dyer, Jeff. "Lessons from Tesla's Approach to Innovation." *Harvard Business Review*. https://hbr.org/2020/02/lessons-from-teslas-approach-to-innovation

2. Offensive

28   "From George Washington to John Trumbull, 25 June 1799." *Founders Online*. https://founders.archives.gov/documents/Washington/06-04-02-0120

29   "The Louisiana Purchase." Monticello.org. https://www.monticello.org/thomas-jefferson/louisiana-lewis-clark/the-louisiana-purchase/

30   "TACTICAL FUNDAMENTALS B2B2269 STUDENT HANDOUT." United States Marine Corps. Basic Officer Course. The Basic School. Pg. 7

31   Martineau, Paris and Matsakis, Louise. "Why It's Hard to Escape Amazon's Long Reach." *Wired*. https://www.wired.com/story/why-hard-escape-amazons-long-reach/

32   Duhigg, Charles. "Is Amazon Unstoppable?" *The New Yorker*. https://www.newyorker.com/magazine/2019/10/21/is-amazon-unstoppable

33   Juncu Maria. "Amazon's Most Important Intensive Growth Strategies." *Performance Magazine*. https://www.performancemagazine.org/amazon-growth-strategies/

34   Duhigg, Charles. "Is Amazon Unstoppable?" *The New Yorker*. https://www.newyorker.com/magazine/2019/10/21/is-amazon-unstoppable

35   Reed, Adam. "NBA steps up its global plans to take basketball to new markets." CNBC. https://www.cnbc.com/2019/01/18/nba-steps-up-its-global-plans-to-take-basketball-to-new-markets.html

36   Bakiny, Prosper Junior. "Here's What Shopify Is Doing to Stay Ahead of Competition." *The Motley Fool.* https://www.fool.com/investing/2019/10/17/heres-what-shopify-is-do-ing-to-stay-ahead-of-compe.aspx

37   "Domino's Pizza, Inc. (DPZ)." *Yahoo! finance.* https://finance.yahoo.com/quote/DPZ/

38   "Domino's Pizza Top 10 Innovations." Aaron Allen & Associates. https://aaronallen.com/blog/dominos-pizza-delivery-technology

3. Mass

39   Holzner, Harold. "Civil War Jekyll and Hyde." *The Chicago Tribune.* https://www.chi-cagotribune.com/news/ct-xpm-1993-07-11-9307110376-story.html

40   Monteith, Sharon (editor). *The Cambridge Companion to the Literature of the American South.* Cambridge University Press. 2013. P. 49.

41   "Nathan Bedford Forrest." History.com. https://www.history.com/topics/american-civil-war/nathan-bedford-forrest

42   "TACTICAL FUNDAMENTALS B2B2269 STUDENT HANDOUT." United States Marine Corps. Basic Officer Course. The Basic School. Pg. 7

43   Colvin, Geoffrey."The Ultimate Manager In a time of hidebound, formulaic thinking, General Electric's Jack Welch gave power to the worker and the shareholder. He built one hell of a company in the process." *Fortune* via *CNN Money.* https://money.cnn.com/maga-zines/fortune/fortune_archive/1999/11/22/269126/index.htm

44   Nocera, Joe. "Was Jack Welch Really That Good?" *Bloomberg Businessweek.* https://www.bloomberg.com/news/articles/2019-06-12/reassessing-jack-welch-s-legacy-after-ge-s-decline-joe-nocera

45   Colvin, Geoffrey."The Ultimate Manager In a time of hidebound, formulaic thinking, General Electric's Jack Welch gave power to the worker and the shareholder. He built one hell of a company in the process." *Fortune* via *CNN Money.* https://money.cnn.com/maga-zines/fortune/fortune_archive/1999/11/22/269126/index.htm

46   Lohr, Steve. "Jack Welch, G.E. Chief Who Became a Business Superstar, Dies at 84." *The New York Times.* https://www.nytimes.com/2020/03/02/business/jack-welch-died.html

47   Belvedere, Matthew J. "Ex-director Ken Langone: GE's 'destruction' happened after Jack Welch and it could now be 'busted up'." CNBC. https://www.cnbc.com/2018/02/28/ken-langone-ge-destruction-happened-after-jack-welch-left-as-ceo.html

48   Schrager, James E. "Three strategy lessons from GE's decline." *Chicago Booth Review*. https://review.chicagobooth.edu/strategy/2019/article/three-strategy-lessons-ge-s-decline

49   Byrne, John A. "Jack Welch successor destroyed GE he inherited." *USA Today*. https://www.usatoday.com/story/opinion/2018/07/15/ge-ceo-welch-oppose-editorials-debates/36895027/

50   Bromels, John. "I Still Can't Believe General Electric Spent More Than $10 Billion for Alstom Power." *The Motley Fool*. https://www.fool.com/investing/2018/09/01/i-still-cant-believe-general-electric-spent-more-t.aspx

51   Ausick, Paul. "Why GE's Alstom Acquisition Was Misguided." *24/7 Wall St*. https://247wallst.com/industrials/2019/06/07/why-ges-alstom-acquisition-was-misguided/

52   Egan, Matt. "How decades of bad decisions broke GE." *CNN Business*. https://money.cnn.com/2017/11/20/investing/general-electric-immelt-what-went-wrong/index.html

53   Dierking, David. "4 Companies Dropped From the Dow." *Investopedia*. https://www.investopedia.com/articles/investing/113015/4-famous-companies-dropped-dow-jones.asp

4. Economy of Force

54   Bauer, Ted. "Stop chasing shiny objects." *Medium*. https://medium.com/@tedbauer2003/stop-chasing-shiny-objects-593af15f5577

55   Malone, Tim. "Real world example of scope creep." *TechRepublic*. https://www.techrepublic.com/blog/tech-of-all-trades/real-world-example-of-scope-creep/

56   Bloom, Peter. "Diversification can be deadly." *Washington Business Journal*. https://www.bizjournals.com/washington/blog/fedbiz_daily/2011/06/diversification-can-be-deadly.html

57   "TACTICAL FUNDAMENTALS B2B2269 STUDENT HANDOUT." United States Marine Corps. Basic Officer Course. The Basic School. Pg. 8

58   Anderson, Gary. "How 'Economy of Force' warfare works and why Trump should use it." *The Washington Times*. https://www.washingtontimes.com/news/2019/oct/30/how-economy-of-force-warfare-works-and-why-trump-s/

59   Boudette, Neal E. "Ford Will Build Electric Cars in Mexico, Shifting Its Plan." *The New York Times*. https://www.nytimes.com/2017/12/07/business/ford-plant-electric.html

60   Mankins, Michael, Harding, David, and Weddigen, Rolf-Magnus. "How the Best Divest." *Harvard Business Review*. https://hbr.org/2008/10/how-the-best-divest

5. Maneuver

61   Higgins, Peter E. "Historical Applications Of Maneuver Warfare In The 20th Century." GlobalSecurity.org. https://www.globalsecurity.org/military/library/report/1990/HPE.htm

62   "Battle of Sidi Barrani." Military.Wikia.Org. https://military.wikia.org/wiki/Battle_of_Sidi_Barrani

63   Higgins, Peter E. "Historical Applications Of Maneuver Warfare In The 20th Century." GlobalSecurity.org. https://www.globalsecurity.org/military/library/report/1990/HPE.htm

64   United States. Department of the Navy. Warfighting. Marine Corps Doctrinal Publication No. 1. (United States Government, 1997), 77-78.

65   "Battle of Chancellorsville." History.com. https://www.history.com/topics/american-civil-war/battle-of-chancellorsville

66   "Battle of Austerlitz." *Encylopaedia Britannica*. https://www.britannica.com/event/Battle-of-Austerlitz

67   "Battle of Austerlitz, 2 December 1805." HistoryOfWar.org. http://www.historyofwar.org/articles/battles_austerlitz.html

68   Hunt, Patrick. "Battle of Cannae." *Encylopaedia Britannica*. https://www.britannica.com/event/Battle-of-Cannae

69   "TACTICAL FUNDAMENTALS B2B2269 STUDENT HANDOUT." United States Marine Corps. Basic Officer Course. The Basic School. Pg. 8

70   Bogost, Ian. "Obama Was Too Good at Social Media." *The Atlantic*. https://www.theatlantic.com/technology/archive/2017/01/did-america-need-a-social-media-president/512405/

71   Nguyen, Tina. "Obama's Social Media Team: 20 Aides, Countless Memes." *Vanity Fair Hive*. https://www.vanityfair.com/news/2015/11/obama-social-media-team

72   Freking, Kevin. "Obama makes his mark as first 'social media' president." The Associated Press via *The Seattle Times*. https://www.seattletimes.com/nation-world/nation-politics/obama-makes-his-mark-as-first-social-media-president/

73   Rutledge, Pamela. "How Obama Won the Social Media Battle in the 2012 Presidential Campaign." *The Media Psychology Blog*. https://mprcenter.org/blog/2013/01/how-obama-won-the-social-media-battle-in-the-2012-presidential-campaign/

74   "How Netflix Became a $100 Billion Company in 20 Years." *Product Habits Blog*. https://producthabits.com/how-netflix-became-a-100-billion-company-in-20-years/

75   "How Netflix Became a $100 Billion Company in 20 Years." *Product Habits Blog*. https://producthabits.com/how-netflix-became-a-100-billion-company-in-20-years/

76   "How Is Southwest Different From Other Airlines?" *Investopedia*. https://www.investopedia.com/articles/investing/061015/how-southwest-different-other-airlines.asp

77   Silk, Robert. "Southwest the top airline in JD Power survey." *Travel Weekly*. https://www.travelweekly.com/Travel-News/Airline-News/Southwest-the-top-airline-in-JD-Power-survey

78   LeBeau, Phil. "Consumer satisfaction in the skies soars to record high in annual airline travel survey." CNBC. https://www.cnbc.com/2019/05/28/consumer-satisfaction-soars-to-record-high-in-airline-travel-survey.html

6. Unity of Command

79   Bowden, Mark. "The Desert One Debacle." *The Atlantic*. https://www.theatlantic.com/magazine/archive/2006/05/the-desert-one-debacle/304803/

80   Kamps, Charles Tustin. "Operation Eagle Claw: The Iran Hostage Rescue Mission." *Air & Space Power Journal*. http://www.airpower.maxwell.af.mil/apjinternational/apj-s/2006/3tri06/kampseng.html

81   "Jimmy Carter Blames Failed Iran Rescue Effort for Defeat to Reagan." The Associated Press via Fox News. http://www.foxnews.com/politics/2010/09/18/jimmy-carter-blames-failed-iran-rescue-effort-defeat-reagan.html

82   "Document 8" (The Holloway Report). The National Security Archive: The George Washington University. http://nsarchive.gwu.edu/NSAEBB/NSAEBB63/doc8.pdf

83   Kreisher, Otto. "Desert One." *Air Force Magazine*. https://www.airforcemag.com/article/0199desertone/

84   Goldwater-Nichols Department of Defense Reorganization Act of 1986. 99th Congress. Public Law 99-433 (Oct. 1, 1986) Historical Office: Office of the Secretary of Defense. http://history.defense.gov/Portals/70/Documents/dod_reforms/Goldwater-NicholsDoDReordAct1986.pdf

85   "TACTICAL FUNDAMENTALS B2B2269 STUDENT HANDOUT." United States Marine Corps. Basic Officer Course. The Basic School. Pg. 9

86   Larcker, David and Tayan, Brian. "The Management of Berkshire Hathaway." Case Studies. The Stanford School of Business. https://www.gsb.stanford.edu/faculty-research/case-studies/management-berkshire-hathaway

87   Lynch, Shana. "What Is It Like to Be Owned by Warren Buffett?" *Insights by Stanford Business*. https://www.gsb.stanford.edu/insights/what-it-be-owned-warren-buffett

88   O'Connell, Brian. History of Berkshire Hathaway: Timeline and Facts. *TheStreet*. https://www.thestreet.com/investing/history-of-berkshire-hathaway

89   Oyedele, Akin. "If you want to work in Berkshire Hathaway's Omaha office, start looking for another job." *Business Insider*. https://www.businessinsider.com/berkshire-hathaway-omaha-office-staff-2016-2

90   Novet, Jordan. "SAP sticks to tradition with dual CEO appointments as McDermott departs." CNBC. https://www.cnbc.com/2019/10/11/sap-maintains-dual-ceo-tradition-as-bill-mcdermott-departs.html

91   "SAP Sets Course for the Future with Next-Generation Leadership Team." SAP SE. https://news.sap.com/2019/10/sap-set-course-future-next-generation-leadership/

92   Miller, Ron. "More than ever, the current environment requires companies to take swift, determined action which is best supported by a very clear leadership structure." *TechCrunch*. https://techcrunch.com/2020/04/21/and-then-there-was-one-co-ceo-jennifer-morgan-to-depart-sap/

93   Grant, Nico. "Software Companies Abandon Co-CEOs, Exposing the Model's Risks." Bloomberg. https://www.bloomberg.com/news/articles/2020-04-22/software-companies-abandon-co-ceos-exposing-the-model-s-risks

94   Dumont, Martin. "4 Biggest Merger and Acquisition Disasters." *Investopedia*. https://www.investopedia.com/articles/financial-theory/08/merger-acquisition-disasters.asp

95   Grocer, Stephen. "What Happened to AOL Time Warner?" *The New York Times*. https://www.nytimes.com/2018/06/15/business/dealbook/aol-time-warner.html

7. Security

96   Gaub, Florence. "Lebanon's civil war: seven lessons forty years on." European Union Institute for Security Studies. https://www.iss.europa.eu/sites/default/files/EUISSFiles/Alert_21_Lebanon_civil_war.pdf

97   "The Reagan Administration and Lebanon, 1981–1984." Office of the Historian. U.S. Department of State. https://history.state.gov/milestones/1981-1988/lebanon

98   The Department of State bulletin. v.82 1982 July-Dec. U.S. Department of State. https://babel.hathitrust.org/cgi/pt?id=mdp.39015077200098&view=1up&seq=451

99   Ernsberger, Richard. "1983 Beirut barracks bombing: 'The BLT Building is gone!'" *Marine Times*. https://www.marinecorpstimes.com/news/your-marine-corps/2019/10/23/1983-beirut-barracks-bombing-the-blt-building-is-gone/

100   "Report of the DOD Commission on Beirut International Airport Terrorist Attack, October 23, 1983." https://fas.org/irp/threat/beirut-1983.pdf

101   "U.S. Marines deployed to Lebanon" History.com. https://www.history.com/this-day-in-history/u-s-marines-deployed-to-lebanon

102   Levitt, Matthew. "Why the CIA Killed Imad Mughniyeh." *Politico*. https://www.politi-co.com/magazine/story/2015/02/mughniyeh-assassination-cia-115049

103   "1993 World Trade Center Bombing Fast Facts." CNN. https://www.cnn.com/2013/11/05/us/1993-world-trade-center-bombing-fast-facts/index.html

104   Tierney, Dominic. "The Twenty Years' War." *The Atlantic*. https://www.theatlantic.com/international/archive/2016/08/twenty-years-war/496736/

105   "TACTICAL FUNDAMENTALS B2B2269 STUDENT HANDOUT." United States Marine Corps. Basic Officer Course. The Basic School. Pg. 8

106   Roberts, Amy and Skjong, Ingrid. "Peloton Review: What to Know Before You Buy." *Wirecutter* from The New York Times. https://www.nytimes.com/wirecutter/reviews/peloton-review-what-to-know-before-you-buy/

107   Patel, Neil. "Is Peloton Building a True Competitive Advantage?" *The Motley Fool*. https://www.fool.com/investing/2020/06/14/is-peloton-building-a-true-competitive-advantage.aspx

108   Brooks, Khristopher J. "24 Hour Fitness declares bankruptcy, citing "devastating" coronavirus hit." CBS News. https://www.cbsnews.com/news/24-hour-fitness-bankruptcy-chapter11-closes-gyms/

109   Muoio, Dave. "iFit raises $200M to stream fitness content on NordicTrack workout machines." *MobiHealthNews*. https://www.mobihealthnews.com/news/ifit-raises-200m-stream-fitness-content-nordictrack-workout-machines

110   van Doorn, Philip. "Opinion: Airlines and Boeing want a bailout — but look how much they've spent on stock buybacks." *MarketWatch*. https://www.marketwatch.com/story/airlines-and-boeing-want-a-bailout-but-look-how-much-theyve-spent-on-stock-buy-backs-2020-03-18

111   Rucinski, Tracy and Shepardson, David. "Airline workers are asking Congress for another $32 billion bailout." Reuters. https://www.businessinsider.com/airline-workers-unions-ask-congress-for-another-32-billion-bailout-2020-6

8. Surprise

112   Michael Handel, "Intelligence and the Problem of Strategic Surprise." *The Journal of Strategic Studies* Vol. 7, No. 3 September 1984, pp. 229-230 https://thecsi.org.uk/isi/wp-content/uploads/2018/07/Intelligence-and-the-problem-of-strategic-surprise.pdf?0856f5

113   Hunt, Patrick. "Battle of Trasimene." *Encyclopaedia Britannica*. https://www.britanni-ca.com/topic/Battle-of-Trasimene

114   Onion, Rebecca. "Washington's 1776 Warning to the City of New York: 'Get Out While You Can.'" *Slate*. https://slate.com/human-interest/2016/10/george-washingtons-1776-evacuation-proclamation-to-the-city-of-new-york.html

115   "10 Facts about Washington's Crossing of the Delaware River." George Washington's Mount Vernon. https://www.mountvernon.org/george-washington/the-revolutionary-war/washingtons-revolutionary-war-battles/the-trenton-princeton-campaign/10-facts-about-washingtons-crossing-of-the-delaware-river/

116   "Battles of Trenton and Princeton." *Encyclopaedia Britannica*. https://www.britannica.com/event/Battles-of-Trenton-and-Princeton

117   Hunt, Patrick. "Quintus Fabius Maximus Verrucosus." *Encyclopaedia Britannica*. https://www.britannica.com/biography/Quintus-Fabius-Maximus-Verrucosus

118   "Crossing of the Delaware." George Washington's Mount Vernon. https://www.mount-vernon.org/library/digitalhistory/digital-encyclopedia/article/crossing-of-the-delaware/

119   "WHAT YOU NEED TO KNOW ABOUT THE BATTLE OF THE BULGE." Imperial War Museum (IWM). https://www.iwm.org.uk/history/what-you-need-to-know-about-the-battle-of-the-bulge

120   "General Patton relieves Allies at Bastogne." History.com. https://www.history.com/this-day-in-history/patton-relieves-bastogne

121   "Battle of Coral Sea." History.com. https://www.history.com/topics/world-war-ii/battle-of-coral-sea

122   "Battle of Midway." History.com. https://www.history.com/topics/world-war-ii/battle-of-midway

123   Miller, Ron. "How AWS came to be." *TechCrunch*. https://techcrunch.com/2016/07/02/andy-jassys-brief-history-of-the-genesis-of-aws/

124   "Announcing Amazon Elastic Compute Cloud (Amazon EC2) - beta." AWS. https://aws.amazon.com/about-aws/whats-new/2006/08/24/announcing-amazon-elastic-compute-cloud-amazon-ec2---beta/

125   Dignan, Larry. "Top cloud providers in 2020: AWS, Microsoft Azure, and Google Cloud, hybrid, SaaS players.' *ZDNet*. https://www.zdnet.com/article/the-top-cloud-providers-of-2020-aws-microsoft-azure-google-cloud-hybrid-saas/

126   Chapel, David. "AWS vs Azure vs Google Cloud Market Share 2020: What the Latest Data Shows." *Medium*. https://medium.com/@jaychapel/aws-vs-azure-vs-google-cloud-market-share-2020-what-the-latest-data-shows-9afd4accf8d7

127   "Annual revenue of Amazon Web Services from 2013 to 2019." *Statista*. https://www.statista.com/statistics/233725/development-of-amazon-web-services-revenue/

128   Duhigg, Charles. Is Amazon Unstoppable? *The New Yorker*. https://www.newyorker.com/magazine/2019/10/21/is-amazon-unstoppable

129   Anderton, Ethan. "Steve Jobs Wanted Bob Iger To Shut Down Disney Animation After Pixar Acquisition." */Film*. https://www.slashfilm.com/walt-disney-animation-almost-shut-down/

130   Anderton, Ethan. "Steve Jobs Wanted Bob Iger To Shut Down Disney Animation After Pixar Acquisition." */Film*. https://www.slashfilm.com/walt-disney-animation-almost-shut-down/

131   Whitten, Sarah. "14 years, 4 acquisitions, 1 Bob Iger: How Disney's CEO revitalized an iconic American brand." CNBC. https://www.cnbc.com/2019/08/06/bob-iger-forever-changed-disney-with-4-key-acquisitions.html

132   "TACTICAL FUNDAMENTALS B2B2269 STUDENT HANDOUT." United States Marine Corps. Basic Officer Course. The Basic School. Pg. 9

9. Simplicity

133   Dalzell, Tom (editor). *The Routledge Dictionary of Modern American Slang and Unconventional English*. 2009. P. 595. https://books.google.com/books?id=5F-YNZRv-VMC&pg=PA595#v=onepage&q&f=false

134   Tim, Alex. "Keep It Simple, Stupid (KISS) Guidelines." *Informatica*. https://blogs.informatica.com/2020/02/07/keep-it-simple-stupid-kiss-guidelines/

135   "KISS (Keep it Simple, Stupid) - A Design Principle." Interactive Design Foundation. https://www.interaction-design.org/literature/article/kiss-keep-it-simple-stupid-a-bfgb-principle

136   "TACTICAL FUNDAMENTALS B2B2269 STUDENT HANDOUT." United States Marine Corps. Basic Officer Course. The Basic School. Pg. 9

137   "F.M.F.M. 1 Warfighting." Clausewitz.com. https://www.clausewitz.com/readings/Warfit1.htm

138   Ettore, Mike. "Friction." *Trust-Based Leadership™: Marine Corps Leadership Concepts for Today's Business Leaders*, 1st ed., ADP, 2019, pp. 237–239.

139   CNN Editorial Research. "Death of Osama bin Laden Fast Facts." CNN. https://www.cnn.com/2013/09/09/world/death-of-osama-bin-laden-fast-facts/index.html

140   "The order that launched the Charge of the Light Brigade, 1854." The National Army Museum. https://collection.nam.ac.uk/detail.php?acc=1962-11-4-3#:~:text=R.,the%20enemy%20had%20captured%20earlier.

141   Greenspan, Jesse. "The Charge of the Light Brigade, 160 Years Ago." History.com. https://www.history.com/news/the-charge-of-the-light-brigade-160-years-ago

142   Carlson, Ben. "Napoleon's Corporal." *A Wealth of Common Sense*. http://awealthof-commonsense.com/2016/04/napoleons-corporal/

143   "Kelly's 14 Rules & Practices." Lockheed Martin. https://www.lockheedmartin.com/en-us/who-we-are/business-areas/aeronautics/skunkworks/kelly-14-rules.html

144   Ashkenas, Ron. "Simplicity-Minded Management." *Harvard Business Review*. https://hbr.org/2007/12/simplicity-minded-management

145   "Simplicity at work." Siegel+Gale. https://www.siegelgale.com/new-siegelgale-study-shows-simple-workplaces-foster-employee-engagement/

Trust-Based Leadership™ Section II

27. Trust

146   United States. Department of the Navy. *Warfighting. Marine Corps Doctrinal Publication No. 1.* (United States Government, 1997), 77-78.

147   "Iraqi Army." GlobalSecurity.org. https://www.globalsecurity.org/military/world/iraq/army.htm (Accessed June 29, 2019)

148   Larcker, David and Tayan, Brian. "The Management of Berkshire Hathaway." Case Studies. The Stanford School of Business. https://www.gsb.stanford.edu/faculty-research/case-studies/management-berkshire-hathaway (Accessed Aug. 18, 2018)

149   Lynch, Shana. "What Is It Like to Be Owned by Warren Buffett?" *Insights by Stanford Business*. https://www.gsb.stanford.edu/insights/what-it-be-owned-warren-buffett (Accessed Aug. 18, 2018)

28. Mission Tactics

150   United States. Department of the Navy. *Warfighting. Marine Corps Doctrinal Publication No. 1.* (United States Government, 1997), 85-86.

151   Higgins, Peter E. "Historical Applications of Maneuver Warfare in the 20th Century." Thesis, USA Command & Staff College, 1990. Retrieved from: https://www.globalsecurity.org/military/library/report/1990/HPE.htm

152   United States. Department of the Navy. *Warfighting.* 88-89.

29. Decentralized Command & Control

153   United States. Department of the Navy. *Warfighting. Marine Corps Doctrinal Publication No.* 1. (United States Government, 1997), 77-78.

154   *Warfighting.* 81

155   Keyur. "A Family of Companies – Johnson & Johnson." Assignment: Technology and Operations Management Course. Harvard Business School. https://rctom.hbs.org/submission/a-family-of-companies-johnson-johnson/ (accessed Aug. 17, 2018)

156   "Johnson & Johnson CEO William Weldon: Leadership in a Decentralized Company." *Knowledge@Wharton.* Wharton University of Pennsylvania. http://knowledge.wharton.upenn.edu/article/johnson-johnson-ceo-william-weldon-leadership-in-a-decentralized-company/ (accessed Aug. 17, 2018)

157   Conlin, Michelle. "The most decentralized company in the world." *Forbes.* https://www.forbes.com/forbes/1999/0111/6301142a.html#a81f3c78292c (accessed Aug. 17, 2018)

158   Lee, Louise. Nicholas Bloom: Decentralized Firms are More Recession-Proof. *Insights by Stanford Business.* https://www.gsb.stanford.edu/insights/nicholas-bloom-decentralized-firms-are-more-recession-proof (accessed Aug. 17, 2018)

159   Note: This is a true story, but some of the details have been changes to protect identities.

31. Simplicity

160   Carlson, Ben. "Napoleon's Corporal." *A Wealth of Common Sense.* http://awealthofcommonsense.com/2016/04/napoleons-corporal/ (Accessed Aug. 18, 2018)

161   The United States Marine Corps Officer Candidates School Training Command. "THE OPERATION ORDER – PART 1 (S.M.E.A.C.)" TACT 3020-1. https://www.usnavy.vt.edu/Marines/PLC_Junior/Fall_Semester/TACT3020_Op_Order1_Student_Outline.pdf (Accessed Aug. 18, 2018)

162   "BREVITY: MULTISERVICE BREVITY CODES." *Marine Corps Reference Publication No. 3-25B.* (United States Government, 2002). http://www.dtic.mil/dtic/tr/fulltext/u2/a404426.pdf (Accessed Aug. 8, 2018)

32. Standard Operating Procedures

163   UNITED STATES MARINE CORPS. "Marine Corps Artillery Fire Support Training Standing Operating Procedures (SOP)." JRegtO P3570.2. http://sill-www.army.mil/usmc/documents/fire_support.pdf (Accessed Aug. 19, 2018)

164   United States. Department of the Navy. *Tactics, Techniques, and Procedures For Fire Support for the Combined Arms Commander*. Marine Corps Resource Publication No. 3-16C. (United States Government, 2002). 21

165   Farber, Betty. "8 Steps to a Successful Sales Call." *Entrepreneur*. https://www.entrepreneur.com/article/207016 (Accessed on Aug. 19, 2018)

34. Friction

166   "FMFM 1 Warfighting." https://www.marines.mil/Portals/1/Publications/MCDP%201%20Warfighting.pdf (Accessed Aug. 19, 2018)

167   United States. Department of the Navy. *Warfighting. Marine Corps Doctrinal Publication No. 1.* (United States Government, 1997), 5-6.

168   Author interview with Marine Corps Special Operator; name and identity withheld by request.

35. Detachment

169   Clausewitz, Carl von. *On War*. Princeton University Press, Princeton, 1976, 101. Via FitzSimons, Peter. "The Fog of War." Penguin.com.au. https://www.penguin.com.au/books/victory-at-villers-bretonneux-9781742759531/article/1088-fog-war (Accessed Aug. 24, 2018)

170   Murray, Seb. "How brain science found its way into business school." *Financial Times*. https://www.ft.com/content/623f049a-1269-11e8-a765-993b2440bd73 (Accessed Aug. 24, 2018)

171   Nauert, Rick. "Stress May Impair Decision-Making." *PsychCentral*. https://psychcentral.com/news/2008/11/21/stress-may-impair-decision-making/3390.html (Accessed Aug. 24, 2018)

172   "Chronic Stress Linked to Mild Cognitive Impairment and Other Health Problems." *University Health News Daily*. https://universityhealthnews.com/daily/depression/chronic-stress-linked-to-mild-cognitive-impairment-and-other-health-problems/ (Accessed Aug. 24, 2018)

36. The Force Multiplier

173   Gatchel, Theodore L. "Gunny, Put Up The Flagpole." *Marine Corps Gazette*.

Printed in Great Britain
by Amazon

39314736R00090